THE FUTURE OF PALESTINE

Bobbi,

If all our pastors were like you, the world would be much more beautiful! I hold so much respect for you. Thank you so much for your support!

THE FUTURE OF PALESTINE

THE FUTURE OF PALESTINE: HOW DISCRIMINATION HINDERS CHANGE

TAMAR HADDAD

NEW DEGREE PRESS

THE FUTURE OF PALESTINE
The Future of Palestine: How Discrimination Hinders Change

ISBN

978-1-63676-635-5 *Paperback*
978-1-63676-218-0 *Kindle Ebook*
978-1-63676-220-3 *Digital Ebook*

EPIGRAPH

——

History repeats itself.
It's what I've heard over and over again.
History repeats itself.
The oppressed becomes the oppressor.
History repeats itself.
This is what should change.

She enjoys watching him die in front of her eyes.

Amid a misty, starless, still night, a khaki uniform appears, looming bigger and bigger from the distant horizon. She notices a shiny black rifle attached to the right side of his uniform. The body wearing the full-on khaki is about eight feet tall. She looks up to see his face better. It aches the back of her neck. She notices his huge teeth that cover half of his face. He slowly leans closer to her and looks down at her. Then, he points his rifle right between her eyes. He doesn't shoot her, and he won't. Shooting her is merciful, and he is ruthless. Instead, he tells her the story of how he murdered her husband. "The first bullet wounded his left foot," he says with a deep, husky voice. "I immobilized your filthy, helpless husband. Yes! He was helpless. And his screams? *I fed* on them," the man in khaki grins in the dark.

A hot drop of sweat hisses on the ground.

"The second bullet paralyzed his hand. He can't write anymore. This time his screams made me even stronger," the man in khaki laughs like a devil.

A sweat drop slowly draws a line on her wrinkly cheek.

"I aimed the last bullet on his heart," he mumbles.

She rapidly opens her black eyes in panic. The darkness fades away. Sweat drops decorate her face like dewdrops on a thorny rose on an early morning. She calls her son Ali. No reply. She calls Omar, her youngest. Again, no reply. Then, the eldest daughter checks on her mother.

"Are you okay, mother? Do you need anything?" The daughter's eyebrows lift. Three horizontal lines appear on her forehead.

"It's just a bad dream. Where are your brothers? Ali? Omar?" The mother calls her boys.

No reply.

"Why aren't they answering me?" The mother's voice cracks.

"They are milking the sheep." The daughter consoles her.

The boys finally enter the modest, isolated house from the rest of the world. The mother and the daughter go to the living room to greet the men. The small, white bricked house has a smooth dome in its center. Arches stand at the entrance of the two bedrooms. It looks like a cave house in the middle of nowhere. It has a few pictures of religious Arabic writings. A couple of big, blue, evil eyes hang on two adjacent walls to protect the house.

Ali orders his sister to make cheese out of the milk he just got.

The sister takes the milk and goes to the tiny, old kitchen.

"Make us breakfast first, you dumb girl," Ali says.

She obeys.

She brings them breakfast to the living room, but she does not sit and eat with them. She goes back to the kitchen and starts making the cheese instead. The mother sits with her boys. She puts a long, black fabric on her lap and some red strings to her right. She continues embroidering a Palestinian dress for herself. There is already a square like patch of red print in the center of the pitch-black fabric.

To the family's surprise, someone unexpectedly knocks on their door. No one has ever knocked on their door ever since they moved to this house a long time ago.

"Could it be dad and—?" asks the daughter.

"How could dad know we're in Jordan now, stupid?" Ali interrupts.

"Your father is probably dead," says the mother in a cold tone of voice. Her poker face stares at the door. Her eyes don't blink.

The first time James saw her, he was captivated by her black-diamond eyes that look nothing like his blue eyes. She was truly a Jasmine; fair, delicate, and beautiful.

He could not move his eyes away from her in their first business meeting. He was annoyed every time someone interrupted him in that first meeting with her: "James. JAMES!" Staring at Jasmine watered his dry soul, but his supervisor warned James from her. Too much water can harm the plant. James' supervisor sent him back to the US, but James had to go back to the Arab world, to Jordan, where his Palestinian dream girl is. He had to talk to Jasmine, and he did. For months, all she said was, "Sir, I cannot talk to you." Or, "Please leave me alone, James." A year later, he went down on his knees and proposed. Her answer froze him and paralyzed his legs. Was he still breathing? Could he ever stand up again?

Omar opens the door. A spooky, red monster-like creature babbles some words Omar does not comprehend. He smacks the door in the creature's face out of fear. Omar's sister runs to the kitchen and brings him water. "Omar? Omar?" she cries and splashes the water in his face.

Despite Yasmeen's strict family, she insists on challenging her family. She wants to prove to them she can be as successful as her father. That's how she becomes the only female journalist in her workspace. Everything goes well until she meets James. She can't like him. Her family won't approve of it. But, her heart disagrees.

Behind the window, the mother sees a man fully covered in blood and mud. He is leaning on the front wall of her house. He's smudging his blood on her white bricks. Maybe Omar saw a monster because he has never seen a blonde man with blue eyes before. However, the mother has seen quite a few of those and, surely, such men do not bring good memories. Omar slowly opens his eyes. His sister hugs him tightly. The mother then opens the door. "What do you want?" she asks in Arabic with a sharp tone. At first, he says words nobody can understand. Then he says, "Help me. Water." He collapses on the floor.

Yasmeen thinks for a very long moment. Her family? Or, herself? She says, "Yes. YES! I wanna marry you." Despite her family's views, her culture, and the traditions of her society, she chooses her heart. She chooses what she believes is good for her. It's difficult for a Muslim woman to marry a Christian man, but she loves James. She takes that extra mile. Eventually, she runs away with him. Away from her family. Away from the restrictive traditions. They live happily together for a couple of months. In this surreal period, Jasmine teaches him Arabic, her language. James is a quick learner. But, good things don't last for too long.

James is in serious need of water and help. He is vulnerable now. He falls on his knees first. His face smashes the ground. He gasps for some air. The daughter is the only one who wants to help the man crucified to the ground, but there is nothing she can do about it. The mother has already made her decision. She kicks him out and enjoys watching him die in front of her eyes.

While lying before the isolated house, his life flashes before his eyes. He does not regret loving Jasmine and coming back to her. He regrets not hiding her well and not being able to protect her from her toxic brothers. His supervisor warned him. He told James her brothers would kill him if he even tries to touch Yasmeen. But, James is not worried about his current bad physical condition anymore. He gave up. He stopped looking for help. He already walked for days in the desert. He ran from the place Jasmine's brothers threw him in after beating him up. He begged them to stop. Not for his sake. For hers. The image of the love of his life, strangled by her brothers for the sake of honor would never leave his mind. "Why survive? What for?" he thinks.

After lying on the ground for sixty-seven minutes, the mother orders the boys saying, "Bury the bloody body away from this house." James' bloody body reminded her of her husband's who had to go back to their home in the Palestinian village. He tried to bring their forgotten baby girl but ended up getting shot by an Israeli soldier. She died alone in his arms and on his dead body.

History repeats itself,
But it shouldn't.

TH

From the Author: This fictional story symbolizes the life of many Palestinians. If you're Palestinian, you can relate. If you're a non-Palestinian, this is an introduction to how Palestinian lives can look. I wrote this fictional story as a student at Bethlehem University for a writing competition after reading Toni Morrison's *Beloved*. *Beloved* discusses the implications of the slave trade and its traumas on Africans. Therefore, the story is a short, Palestinian adaptation of Morrison's text and writing style, specifically the idea of two stories overlapping in one text.

To Israa Ghrayeb and every persecuted Palestinian

TABLE OF CONTENTS

———

PREFACE

———

I grew up in a conservative household in the Palestinian society. In my society, believing in God differently and questioning the application of religion is threatening. In my society, rejecting patriarchy is threatening. In my society, supporting the Black Lives Matter movement is threatening. In my society, having queer and nonbinary friends is threatening. On a global scale, defying capitalism is threatening. Questioning the inhumanity of Israel is threatening. Through critical analysis, I will introduce you to the possibility that our perceived differences should not be threatening but instead be welcomed and encouraged.

I have a degree in English Language and Literature from Bethlehem University (BU), where I've learned to think critically and question everything. As I publish this book, I am also studying Music and Entrepreneurship at California Lutheran University (CLU). The Evangelical Lutheran Church in America (ELCA) and CLU are fully covering my scholarship through the International Women Leaders program (IWL). I am blessed to be part of this supportive, diverse, and international family of young women from nineteen different countries in 2020.

To supplement my education, I have benefited from my involvement in some phenomenal leadership programs, including the Middle East Partnership Initiative Student Leaders Program (MEPI-SLP) and the Clinton Global Initiative University (CGIU). Student requirements in both programs include the creation and implementation of their own projects. Each project has a positive impact and makes a change in our communities.

I am currently still developing Yalla—Palestinian Student Leaders, a program that expands the leadership of Palestinian students. The program consists of four main parts:

1. Classes that target marginalized groups

2. Leadership training sessions

3. Community Engagement Plans (CEP): Every student is expected to design and implement their project that brings change

4. Traveling and experiencing diversity through interactions

I aspire to make this program a nonprofit after raising enough funds.

Some of us lack empathy and project inhumanity towards the Other. The Other does not have the power. They are perceived as inferior to the superior one. The Other is the person perceived as lacking. They are the marginalized. And it has always bothered me. Through the leadership shaped in the four elements previously mentioned, my dream is that we become more tolerant of one another. Yalla—Palestinian Student Leaders is planned to launch in the summer of 2021 in Bethlehem, Palestine.

This book is divided into three main parts:

- **Part 1** depicts the Palestinian daily life and history. It tells the Palestinian experience to Non-Palestinians who may be interested in learning about the untold points of view. Western media, for example, may not portray this side of the story. When illustrated, the Palestinian picture is usually stereotypical and not objective, and the Palestinian voice is unheard.

- **Part 2** is mainly for Palestinians. It questions Palestinian/Arab traditions and beliefs on gender, religion, race, and sexual orientation. Additionally, it explains the need to change through the readings of multiple critical theories.

- **Part 3** is directed to all readers. It urges having a positive impact and paying it forward. It shows readers how to achieve change.

Non-Palestinians who are interested in knowing more about the Palestinian culture will find Part 2 particularly interesting. Palestinians are encouraged to read Part 1 for a critical analysis of the Palestinian identity.

INTRODUCTION

———

I was studying in the US when her pictures swarmed the internet. To the rest of the world, she was a headline. "A twenty-one-year-old Palestinian murdered for 'Honor.'" Merriam Webster defines honor killing as, "The traditional practice in some countries of killing a family member who is believed to have brought shame on the family."[1] However, to me, she was Israa, my classmate, my English grammar study partner, and my friend.

"The exam was easy, right? How did you answer question number three though?"

That is what I remember her saying on repeat with her voice jarring my ears, but I can only hear it in my head now. I will never be able to hear her talking to me again.

We were both English majors at Bethlehem University (BU), and we ended up taking the freshman-level grammar requirement as upperclassmen. That class was such a piece of cake for

———

1   *Merriam Webster*, s.v. "Honor Killing," accessed September 25, 2020.

her that the energetic freshmen would surround and bombard her with their unlimited questions on English grammar. Every time, she gladly answered all of their questions. Their youthful, lively eyes sparkled.

Israa was a goddess. A glamorous, hardworking, independent woman who supported her family through her small makeup business. All she wanted was to enjoy spending some time with her fiancé publicly without having to hide her Instagram and Snapchat stories from her cousin, Reham. Hiding some content from family members on social media is not new to many Arab women who fear the judgment of a corrupt patriarchal society.

One day, Israa decided to be rationally brave. She went out with her fiancé to a restaurant, with his sister, in broad daylight. Israa's parents were aware of it. But, not everyone in the family was thrilled about it. When her cousin, Reham, found that out by viewing Israa's story from a mutual friend, Reham accused Israa of having a bad reputation. In a WhatsApp voice message, a messaging application, Reham condemned Israa. She commented on Israa's makeup and the way she acted and dressed. The cousin then questioned the "free" being of Israa saying, "We're all going to die one day," foreshadowing Israa's catastrophic ending.[2]

In those WhatsApp voice notes, Israa desperately tried defending herself to her cousin, who was slut-shaming her. "My father raised me well, and I never do anything behind his back. He

---

2   Israa Ghrayeb, "التسجيلات الصوتية المحذوفة - بين اسراء غريب وبنت عمها ريهام وشو انحكى على بنت عمها؟," Nour Al Kaddah, Aug 31, 2019, YouTube video, 2:42

knows everything. *He knows everything!*" Israa's voice cracked. "My mom knows [my fiancé and his sister] picked me up. My mom is right in front of me, and she knows. Right, mom?"

"Yes," her mother whispers in the background.

"Yes, she's saying yes. Say it louder!" Israa fights for her life.

"*Yes!*"[3]

Israa was sad because even when she came in with "a pure, white heart" and told her cousin, "I love you all and trust you," Reham and her family broke that unspoken trust. Her family members spat their venom, and Israa's white heart turned into a white flag. Many commented on Reham's jealousy of Israa's independence and her capability of financially supporting her family. Reham chose to convince her own father to talk to Israa's dad about this supposedly shameful act. This is where things went wrong for Israa. Israa was then repeatedly beaten by three men in her family, her two brothers and brother-in-law, which consequently destroyed her respiratory system and traumatized her.[4] Until today, her screams heard on all social media platforms while she was in the hospital still haunt me, and I hope they haunt her murderers too.

Imagine you are Israa. Your family believes you are innocent. Blindly fed the idea of "this is the right way to do things," they still choose to beat you.

---

3   Ibid.

4   Muhammed Wattad, "النائب العام الفلسطيني: إسراء غريب قتلت نتيجة الضرب," *Arab 48*, September 12, 2019.

On her deathbed, Israa posted on her Snapchat story, "I am so sorry to say I will have to cancel all the makeup appointments for this month and the following one. I am in a critical situation at the hospital. My spine is broken, and I'm having surgery today. If all goes well, I will keep you updated. If things go wrong, I would have to cancel all the other appointments."

Israa never mentioned why she was in the hospital. The physical and mental abuse wouldn't be assumed by those who were not close to her.

Israa died.

What bothers me the most is not the fact that even her brother-in-law, who is not related to her by blood, had the power to punish her for her acts. What bothers me the most is not the fact she died in vain and for a silly reason. What bothers me the most is not the fact her cunning cousin was the one who snitched on her. After all, I thought blood was thicker than water. What bothers me the most isn't the argument the suspects used in court. That Israa is possessed by a Djinn—a supernatural being. Surprisingly, it is considered a valid claim. What bothers me the most is that Israa could have made some real change in her life rather than death. Israa had a lot of potentials she could have utilized to make real changes in the world.

Even though the book starts with the heart-wrenching story of Israa, it does not end there. And it is not just women who are Othered in Palestinian society. Persecution takes place due to the lack of tolerance of people from different religions, beliefs, race, sexual orientation, and class. Palestinians themselves are marginalized when it comes to the bigger political picture. Thus, it is time to make a change by accepting anyone different rather than discriminating against them.

* * *

Currently, Palestine has a population of five million people who have different points of view.[5] According to the General Union of Palestinian Women, in 2019 alone, "At least eighteen Palestinian women have been killed in 'crimes of honor.'"[6] Unfortunately, honor killing is not yet criminalized. In Palestine, when it comes to "abuses inflicted upon women, laws are still considered major sources of women's oppression."[7]

On a larger scale, wars and mass killings committed in the name of religion are due to an extreme misinterpretation of religions' real message of universal love—for example, ISIL, the Crusades, and Israel. In the US, "Black men are about 2.5 times more likely to be killed by police over their life course than are white men. Black women are about 1.4 times more likely to be killed by police than are white women."[8] The persecution of Afro-Palestinians also occurs in Palestine.

---

5   Palestinian Central Bureau of Statistics, الفلسطينيون في نهاية عام 2018 (The State of Palestine: PCBS, 2018), 19.

6   Ali Sawafta, "Palestinian Women Demand Legal Protection after Suspected 'Honor Killing,'" *Reuters*, September 4, 2019.

7   Nadera Shalhoub-Kevorkian, "Femicide and the Palestinian Criminal Justice System: Seeds of Change in the Context of State Building?" *Law & Society Review* 36, no. 3 (2002): 577.

8   Frank Edwards, Hedwig Lee, and Michael Esposito. "Risk of Being Killed by Police Use of Force in the United States by Age, Race–Ethnicity, and Sex," *PNAS*, August 20, 2019.

When it comes to the disapproval of the LGBTQIA+ community,

- "LGB youth seriously contemplate suicide at almost three times the rate of heterosexual youth."

- "LGB youth are almost five times as likely to have attempted suicide compared to heterosexual youth."

- "In [an American] study, forty percent of transgender adults reported having made a suicide attempt. Ninety-two percent of these individuals reported having attempted suicide before the age of twenty-five."

- "Each episode of LGBT victimization, such as physical or verbal harassment or abuse, increases the likelihood of self-harming behavior by 2.5 times on average."[9]

Despite the legal acceptance of the LGBTQIA+ community in some countries, this community is still widely rejected by many Palestinians.

Lastly, approximately "ten percent of the world lives in extreme poverty, surviving on $1.90 a day or less,"[10] and the percentage is increasing due to the coronavirus.[11]

---

9   "Facts About Suicide," *The Trevor Project*, September 20, 2017, accessed June 14, 2020.

10 Andrea Peer, "Global Poverty: Facts, FAQs, and How to Help," *World Vision*, June 11, 2020.

11 "Poverty: Overview," *World Bank*, April 16, 2020, accessed September 15, 2020.

The tradition goes like this: Become a doctor, an engineer, or a lawyer, and you will be somebody. Everyone will respect you. Yet, the same people who believe in this can be misogynist, racist, or homophobic. At least those I know. Some would see doctors, engineers, and lawyers as the promising people of a traditional society. But it is not about tradition versus modernity. It is about what they give to society. It is about their morality. It is about being humane. It is about accepting diversity.

To be tolerant, one has to think critically and look for deeper meanings through various critical lenses. Do not take things for granted. Just because you believe your religion condones an action or supports a tradition does not necessarily mean that your religion, in its purest form, truly condones the act. You should consider the human aspect of those traditions. But why religion?

"Religion is being used as an excuse to discriminate against and harm others."[12] Some tend to ignore the fact that messengers and prophets wrote the Holy Books in a different time and culture. On the contrary, religion's purpose is to encourage people to be better human beings, yet people choose to interpret it according to their needs. When you question given beliefs, that is when you ultimately become a better leader.

* * *

Sometimes, I sit down and try to write. Not a single word comes out. Yet, when I think of the unfairness of the world

---

12 ACLU, "End the Use of Religion to Discriminate," *American Civil Liberties Union*, May 19, 2016.

we live in, my keyboard rattles. This book speaks about the unspoken, celebrates the marginalized, humanizes the disposed of, and helps you make a change.

By and large, Palestinians suffer every day and lack basic human rights due to the Israeli occupation. But let us not ignore the inhumanities within Palestine and between Palestinians themselves. Some Palestinians persecute the Other, minorities, or different people within Palestine. Through post-colonial, psychoanalytical, nationalist, feminist, racial, queer, philosophical, and Marxist readings, Palestinians should be able to comprehend why social tolerance is vital. Besides, the expectation of anyone who reads the book is for them to pay it forward. Make at least one change, no matter how small, that positively impacts someone or your community. The end goal is to eliminate the discrimination and persecution of those who are different.

Changing the world is not as impossible as it seems if it starts with you! It does not have to revolve around donating and developing social programs and nongovernmental organizations. It can be as simple as changing your mindset about a stereotypical idea you have of someone. Thus, let us embrace change.

I kindly ask all readers to have an open mind.

PART I

THE PALESTINIAN-ISRAELI CONFLICT

CHAPTER ONE

ONE STORY, TWO PROTAGONISTS

———

"Close all windows!"

It's 3 a.m. and my mom is in war mode. Her pursuit of the source of a floor-rattling noise has propelled her through the darkened halls of our three-bedroom house. And now, she is standing at my bedside in the bedroom I have shared with my two younger sisters.

"Are you girls okay?"

I have my t-shirt pulled up over my face and dare not uncover my mouth to speak.

"What just happened?" coughing and gasping for air, my sister asks.

"It's tear gas bombs," Mom tells us. I hear her slippers shuffle toward our window, overlooking the street where my dad first taught me to ride a bike. "Thank God they didn't shatter your windows," she adds.

Thank God my strong, old-fashioned shutters are down, I tell myself today as I replay the memories in my mind. They are as clear now as they were almost five years ago, on the night military tanks rumbled into my family's Arab neighborhood.

"Yo! Tamar!" It was my friend, classmate, and neighbor in a blurry Facebook message. I remember picking up my phone that night, hoping to find out what was going on outside. "Is the smell as bad on your side of the street?" my friend asks.

"Yeah! What do they want?" I text back and describe the scene inside my house." My mom, sister, and I are checking out the tanks right in front of our apartment. So far, I can tell three Israeli soldiers are roaming our block.

"They are looking for someone in the next block," he says in his reply.

They are IDF soldiers. Israel Defense Forces. *They* are part of life for Palestinians.

"They are actually running surveillance on the roof of your building right now!" he writes again.

IDF remained in the area for two more hours, threw at least five more tear gas bombs, and took one hostage. What they did not do, however, was capture the one Palestinian guy they had been searching for from the vantage point of our rooftop.

No more flashbacks. No more trauma. Even in my present, such events excite me rather than scare me. It is peculiar, but my body has gone numb. This is a glimpse of what it is like to be a Palestinian. Yet, every Palestinian has a different story. Every person has a different story. And stories tend to have their protagonists and antagonists. For some stories, the two sides are truth and falsehood. Therefore, this chapter opens the door to the Palestinian-Israeli conflict starting with the history of Jews and their persecution, followed by the Palestinian Diaspora.

THE PERSECUTION OF JEWS

Throughout history, Jews have been severely persecuted. Introduced to anti-Semitism after World War I (1914–1918), Adolf Hilter reached the peak of his discrimination against the Jews in Nazi Germany in World War II (1939–1945).[13] Due to his toxic nationalism, he believed that he, Germans, Europeans, or white people are of the superior race. Consequently, everyone else would be considered inferior and shall die. At least that was his logical explanation of things—scientific facts do not support this theory.

The Holocaust ruthlessly killed millions of Jews in addition to other minorities at the time in Nazi Germany. According to the Holocaust Encyclopedia, other than the six million Jews,

> The Roma and Sinti were viewed as the 'Gypsy nuisance,' a racially 'inferior' people with criminal habits. Up to 250,000 from across Europe were killed.

---

13   "Why Did Hitler Hate the Jews?" *Anne Frank House*, June 8, 2020, accessed September 16, 2020.

Germans with mental and physical disabilities were considered 'useless eaters' and 'racially defective.' 250,000 were killed.

Poles were viewed as 'subhuman' Slavs. They suffered a brutal German occupation. Tens of thousands of members of the Polish elites were killed or imprisoned as potential leaders of the Polish resistance.

Captured Soviet soldiers were viewed as 'subhuman' Slavs....3.3 million Soviet soldiers died in executions or through intentional starvation and mistreatment.

...Real and suspected political opponents, Jehovah's Witnesses, men accused of engaging in homosexual acts, and persons considered to be 'asocial'...were among the hundreds of thousands of victims who were imprisoned and killed in concentration camps. They died from starvation, disease, overwork, mistreatment, or outright murder.[14]

As for the six million Jews, they were targeted for murder because they were also considered subhuman aliens. White Germans believed Jews were a threat to the pure German blood and race. Thus, their eradication was suspected to be the "final solution to the Jewish Question in Europe."[15]

---

14   *Holocaust Encyclopedia, s.v.* "Who were the Victims?" accessed September 16, 2020.

15   Ibid.

According to Albert Einstein, who was trying to prove one of his important theories that could save the world, the world was going crazy. It seemed like everyone was brainwashed by the idea of patriotism.[16] It was similar to when the coronavirus started, and the world stopped for the first few months to discuss one thing and one thing only, the coronavirus. For example, the main focus of the *news* was the virus and almost nothing else at first.

Persecuted Jews wanted their state in Europe even before Hitler. They were seen as a threat to the economy according to Theodor Herzl in his book, *The Jewish State*, published in 1896.[17] They wanted their own home, land, and government. Thus, on November 2, 1917, a date I, as a Palestinian, will never forget, Arthur Balfour, the foreign minister of Britain, declared the Jewish people would have their state in Palestine. What we know today as the Balfour Declaration reads,

> His Majesty's government view with favor the establishment in Palestine of a national home for the Jewish people, and will use their best endeavors to facilitate the achievement of this object, it being clearly understood that nothing shall be done which may prejudice the civil and religious rights of existing non-Jewish communities in Palestine, or the rights and political status enjoyed by Jews in any other country.[18]

---

16 National Geographic, "National Geographic Documentary 2015. Albert Einstein. How I See the World," World Documentaries, April 8, 2015, YouTube video, 1:34:02.

17 Theodor Herzl, *The Jewish State* (New York: Dover Publications, Inc., 2008), 95.

18 Geoffrey Dawson, "Palestine for the Jews," *The Times of London*, November 9, 1917.

Thus, Britain became the very first world power to endorse this establishment of the Jewish state in Palestine. Britain was one of the first countries to support the Zionist movement. The movement romanticizes the idea of Israel as a Jewish response to anti-Semitism. These few words of Balfour were the very first step for a Jewish hope and a Palestinian Diaspora.

According to Herzl in *The Jewish State*, Jews in Europe lived in ghettos like displaced camps. They were boycotted and needed a space free of persecution, where people are not "openly anti-Semitic."[19] For example, "don't buy from Jews," threatened the Jewish business and economy.[20] Herzl starts a revolutionary movement by saying, "We shall live at last as free men on our own soil, and die peacefully in our own homes. The world will be freed by our liberty, enriched by our wealth, magnified by our greatness."[21]

The founder of Zionism, Herzl, refused the idea of transporting Jews to another country. He believed if they succeeded there, the original people of the land would end up being anti-Semitic as well. He planned to create a new state in either Argentina or Palestine. He says,

> The creation of a new State is neither ridiculous nor impossible. We have in our day witnessed the process in connection with nations which were not largely members of the middle class, but poorer, less educated, and consequently weaker than ourselves. The

---

19   Theodor Herzl, *The Jewish State*, 86.

20   Theodor Herzl, *The Jewish State*, 85.

21   Theodor Herzl, *The Jewish State*, 157.

governments of all countries scourged by anti-Semitism will be keenly interested in assisting us to obtain the sovereignty we want.[22]

Herzl then gives his people the options,

> Shall we choose Palestine or Argentine? Argentine is one of the most fertile countries in the world, extends over a vast area, has a sparse population, and a mild climate. The Argentine Republic would derive considerable profit from the cession of a portion of its territory to us. The present infiltration of Jews has certainly produced some discontent, and it would be necessary to enlighten the Republic on the intrinsic difference of our new movement.[23]

Fertile land is necessary for an agricultural business. After all, his main goal was reviving the Jewish business. The other option was Palestine.

He says,

> Palestine is our ever memorable historic home. The very name of Palestine would attract our people with a force of marvelous potency. If His Majesty the Sultan were to give us Palestine, we could in return undertake to regulate the whole finances of Turkey. We should there form a portion of a rampart of Europe against Asia, an outpost of civilization

---

22   Theodor Herzl, *The Jewish State*, 93.

23   Theodor Herzl, *The Jewish State*, 96.

as opposed to barbarism. We should, as a neutral State, remain in contact with all Europe, which would have to guarantee our existence. The sanctuaries of Christendom would be safeguarded by assigning to them an extra-territorial status, such as is well-known to the law of nations. We should form a guard of honor about these sanctuaries, answering for the fulfillment of this duty with our existence. This guard of honor would be the great symbol of the solution of the Jewish Question after eighteen centuries of Jewish suffering.[24]

Palestine has never been free throughout history. When Herzl started writing his book, Palestine was under Ottoman rule. However, once it fell under the British mandate, Jews could finally have their independent state.

Following that, huge ships carrying thousands of undocumented Jewish immigrants from Europe started entering Palestine under the British mandate publicly. The first wave of immigrants started in 1934, so before WWII. The second wave was during the war, and the third was after Victory in Europe (VE) Day of May 8, 1945. The biggest number of Jewish immigrants from Europe was after the UN partition resolution.

Ilan Pappé, a Jewish historian and social activist born in Haifa, spoke at my high school and described his experience to us. He said, "When the Jews first came to Palestine in ships, they were told that this land, Palestine, had no people."

---

24 Ibid.

When these immigrants landed, they were shocked to see a land with people and a whole civilization of which no one had told them.

The quest is not over. Jewish people did not officially have their independent state then. In 1948, David Ben Gurion, who later became the first prime minister of Israel, was the executive head of the World Zionist Organization and the Chairman of the Jewish Agency for Palestine. On May 14 of the same year, he declared the establishment of the Jewish state of Israel. On that day, and with an agreement with the British, the British left Palestine. The Israeli flag was raised over Palestinian land.

Jewish people finally established a Jewish state. They completed their quest for a Jewish land. Europeans supposedly did not persecute them anymore. Everyone was happy, right?

How would another narration look?

COUNTERPOINT

I have grown up to stories of heroes against villains. In most cases, it is the heroes' narrative. Protagonists usually victimize themselves to gain the sympathy of the readers or the viewers. However, is it really about victims versus monsters? Every side can be monstrous despite the inhumanities they face. I am not trying to victimize Palestinians. Rather, I am just presenting facts.

Because the claim used to create the State of Israel is purely religious, it has not been easy for Palestinians to differentiate between Jews and Israelis for the longest time. For example, I grew up believing, "If you're Israeli, you're a Jew," until I could differentiate Semitism and Zionism. Unfortunately, that is the same reason why Palestinians receive accusations of anti-Semitism. Speaking about their rights can indicate anti-Semitism.

Part of my knowledge about this topic came from traveling. In traveling, I have learned others do not have to worry about water or electricity shortage. I have learned others could travel without any restrictions. I reminisce about being on top of the Zugspitze mountain on the border between Germany and Austria when I was fifteen years old. I was in this huge, circular, wooden restaurant of many layers on the peak of the mountain. Its glass walls portrayed the snowy view of Zugspitze. One of the friends I was with told me, "I'm sitting on the Austrian side." I was on the German side. I thought, *This is crazy!* It made me question my living circumstances back home. It even changed my conception of freedom, the freedom of movement, and living.

* * *

Living in constant war is part of Palestinian life, and the world normalizes it. It started at the beginning of ages. Palestine was doomed to be under constant rule. Throughout history, "Assyrians, Babylonians, Persians, Greeks, Romans, Arabs, Fatimids, Seljuk Turks, Crusades, Egyptians, Mamelukes, and Islamists" ruled Palestine.[25] The Ottoman Empire ruled

---

25 History.com Editors. "Palestine," *History,* A&E Television Networks, August 11, 2017.

Palestine for about 400 years until the British took control of it in 1918 after World War I. Then, The League of Nations issued a British mandate for Palestine, a document that gives Britain the responsibility of establishing a Jewish national homeland in Palestine. Things get uglier in 1947 when the United Nations proposed the Partition Plan of Palestine into two sections. The first is an independent Jewish state and the second is an independent Arab state. Jerusalem would be an internationalized territory.[26]

The moment the last British troops had left Palestine, the British flag came down. Palestinians cheered and danced, but they were oblivious. It was just the beginning of another pain. Seconds later, the Israeli flag hovered over Palestine. It was the moment Palestinians realized they are stuck in a loop and will never see their country free again. They will never see their flag raised high in their land, but they choose to fight for it.

Remember May 15, 1948? The Independence Day for Israel. The same date becomes a Nakba, a catastrophe, a diaspora for Palestinians. Due to Al-Nakba of 1948, about 700,000 to 900,000 Palestinians fled or forcefully left their homes.[27] Neighboring Arab countries emphasized that Palestinians would be able to come back to their homeland once they defeated Israel. Hence, Palestinians kept their house key with them, and the key became a symbol for their hypothetical return. Will they ever return? They are mostly refugees in nearby Arab countries now. Someone else resides in their house.

---

26 Ibid.

27 Ibid.

It did not stop there. Palestine then lost more people and land. Another war took place in 1967, Al-Naksa. Israel gained more land leaving Palestinians with the West Bank and Gaza Strip. Today, Palestinian lands are barely evident on the map. Even inside the West Bank, Israeli settlements are frequently and rapidly built. The US embassy moved to West Jerusalem; thus, Jerusalem became the Capital of Israel. The main goal is to erase Palestine from the face of the Earth. It is working despite the Palestinian resistance.

History showed me that Palestinians are such unlucky people. For them, war becomes normalized. Being stripped from basic human rights is normalized. Living in camps in their land becomes normalized. World powers supporting Israel and demonizing Palestinians become normalized.

THE DAILY LIFE OF A PALESTINIAN

To be a Palestinian comes with consequences: lacking basic human rights every day.

Groups from all over the world visit Bethlehem University to learn about the Palestinian-Israeli conflict. As a BU student and participant in the university's ambassador program, I had the honor of meeting several of those groups and answering their questions. In one of the American groups, a touring guest asked how it felt to be a Palestinian. I remember my friend, who had recently come back from her study abroad in the US, answering that question. She said, "It's ironic how the biggest issue my American friends faced was the best type of mustard that goes best with hot dogs." She added, "It seemed so important for them to argue about it."

The reason why I share this story is that some millennials and even Generation Z in many parts of the Western World are privileged enough not to experience our problems. I am not minimizing their problems because they have their problems. But, living in the US for three years now I realized, it could be difficult for some of my American counterparts to put themselves in my shoes. Therefore, some of them chose to support capitalist Israel. Generally speaking, it is not the expectation that colonizers put themselves in the colonized shoes, but they chose to support other colonizers. And when a Westerner chooses to be pro-Palestine, they are most likely accused of being anti-Semitic. However, people tend to forget that the Israeli government and Jewish people are two different things. On the one hand, many Palestinians persecute Palestinian Jews. On the other hand, there are many Israelis who are pro-Palestine, and likewise, they can face persecution by other Israelis.

I wanted to know why most people in other parts of the world don't experience what Palestinians experience. As a Palestinian, it always seemed normal to drive back home from school under the loud thundering of shells, through tear gas slithering through my nostrils and into my lungs, amongst young Palestinians covering their faces with their Kaffiyehs—throwing rocks at the separation wall ahead, infront of Israeli soldiers pointing their rifles at my bare bodies, and next to tires on fire blocking my way out of this inferno of a crimson-red sky.

I would normally be in the car with some members of my family. Our only shields are the glass windows of the car. My concern and the only thought going through my head would usually be, *When will there be a way out of this mess? I have an exam tomorrow, and I need to study. It's getting late.* I would also think, *Crossing the checkpoint on normal days already takes a lot of time. Now, it's taking an extra hour or two!*

With time, I have realized such incidents shouldn't be what defines me as a Palestinian. I have studied on three other different continents: North America, Europe, and Asia. In none of them have I experienced school going on a strike for political reasons except in Palestine. During the first and second Intifada (a series of Palestinian protests against the Israeli occupation) of 1987 and 2000, educational institutions shut down.

"My dad had to drop out of college," I recall one of my high school classmates saying regarding the first Intifada. "He couldn't afford to wait for life to go back to normal. He had to support his family, so he ended up working as a waiter instead. It was the only job he could get then," she explained.

In America, one can make a decent amount of money as a waiter because tipping is common, yet it isn't in Palestine. My classmate added, "It cost him his entire career." Unfortunately, it is not that different these days either. I remember BU going on a strike every time one of its students got arrested for political reasons. It is a form of protesting against the Israeli occupation.

Palestinians also suffer deprivation of control over their water and air. According to *The Water Accords of Oslo II: Averting a Looming Disaster,*

> Article forty also called for the Palestinian population of West Bank and Gaza to receive 28.6 mcm/y

in additional water for domestic use during the interim period. From its water system, Israel committed to supplying the Palestinians 9.5 mcm/y, including 5 mcm/y for Gaza. However, this water would be sold to Palestinians at the real commercial rate rather than the subsidized rate paid by Israeli consumers. The remainder was to be developed by the PA from the eastern aquifer. Both sides agreed that the total future need of the Palestinians in the West Bank would come to between seventy and eighty mcm/y for both domestic and agricultural use. While it was agreed that this supply was to be developed by the Palestinians from the eastern aquifer and from other West Bank sources to be negotiated in the final-status treaty, the means by which they were to be developed was not addressed in the agreement.[28]

The above reveals that Palestinians are not allowed to dig deep enough into the ground to get their water. Instead, they buy it from Israel.

As for the airspace, the assassinated former president of Palestine Yasser Arafat, opened a domestic airport in Gaza during his presidency. However, it didn't last long.

The state of Palestine has an airline, but not a single airport. Palestinian Airlines was founded in 1995 and started operating on July 23, 1997 with a series

---

28 Alwyn R Rouyer, "The Water Accords of Oslo II: Averting a Looming Disaster, " *Middle East Policy Council* 7, no. 1 (1999).

of flights from Al Arish in Egypt, to Jordan, Saudi Arabia, and the UAE.

In 1998, the airlines started operating in Gaza until forcibly moved again to Al Arish in December 2001 after the attack on the only Palestinian domestic airport by the state of Israel.[29]

The disengagement plan implemented in 2005 states, "Israel will hold sole control of Gaza airspace and will continue to carry out military activities in the waters of the Gaza Strip'...The Oslo Agreements Israel gave Israel full control over Gaza's airspace."[30]

B'tselem documents, after the outbreak of the second intifada (2000), "Israel closed down the airport, and it has not opened since. In December 2001, the Israeli Air Force bombed the airport's runways. From the beginning of the second intifada to the completion of the disengagement plan in 2005, the airport served as an Israeli military base."[31] When the Israeli soldiers left and after the implementation of the disengagement plan, soldiers at the base destroyed and vandalized the buildings.[32]

Luckily, I was born in Jerusalem and I was granted the blue ID that allows me to move more freely than other Palestinians

---

29 Sarah Ahmed Shawky, "Once Upon a Time, Palestine Had Its Own Int'l Airport ... but It Was Short-Lived," *StepFeed*, April 12, 2017, accessed September 16, 2020.

30 "Israel's Control of the Airspace and the Territorial Waters of the Gaza Strip," B'Tselem, accessed September 18, 2020.

31 Ibid.

32 Ibid.

born in the West Bank and Gaza. West Bankers and Gazans have the green ID, which prevents them from moving within the Israeli territories. They would need to apply for a visa-like permit to do so. Unless one has a valid reason, this permit isn't easily issued. An example of a valid reason is hospitalization in Israel since Palestinian hospitals lack the resources.

Palestinians with a green ID cannot even travel from Ben-Gurion's Airport in Tel Aviv. However, I can because of my blue ID, yet that does not mean I have an Israeli passport. As a Jerusalemite, I have a Jordanian passport even when I am not Jordanian. Only people in the West Bank and Gaza have a Palestinian passport. As there isn't any Palestinian airport because of Israel's control of airspace, for them to travel internationally, they would have to cross the Jordanian bridge, Sheikh Hussein.

Another big issue Palestinians experience every day is the lack of mobilization and Israel's control of Palestinian ground. The worst type of immobility comes in the form of checkpoints separating the Israeli and Palestinian territories. I always hear Palestinians say,

"It's a means for them to humiliate us every day."

To go to school, I had to cross the 300 Checkpoint every day between Jerusalem and Bethlehem. Let me tell you. It is not a pleasant experience. It would normally take fifteen minutes to go from Jerusalem to Bethlehem without traffic and checkpoints. However, with the checkpoint, it takes about an hour. At the checkpoint, Israeli soldiers check your blue ID and search the car. Normal people going to school or work might have a bomb in their car. Green ID holders can't cross the checkpoint unless they have a permit. They must step out of the car and go to an airport-like security area with a long line of other people waiting for their turn to be physically searched.

Every Palestinian gets humiliated at the checkpoint. One time, a relative of mine and his family were spending Christmas Eve with his friends in Bethlehem. On their way back home to Jerusalem, he was stopped at the checkpoint. The Israeli soldier at the checkpoint asked my relative to open the window more so he could see my relative's wife. My relative, a typical Middle Eastern man, refused, but what the soldier asked for is considered culturally inappropriate and humiliating. Because my relative refused to further open the car's window so that the soldier sees his beautiful wife, the soldier grabbed him from the car, pinned his face to the dirty ground, and pointed the rifle to his head. His two young children were in the backseat of the car distraught, confused, and terrified.

I was humiliated at checkpoints too. Sometimes, I had to use the public bus to go back and forth from my house to school. At the checkpoint, everybody on the bus, except foreigners, has to step out of the bus. We have to show our IDs to the Israeli soldiers. Foreigners were allowed to stay on the bus because there is no intention to humiliate them, only Palestinians. I was often late to my classes.

The saddest part for me was when my other friend from Jerusalem, Jowana, and I wanted to take our West banker friends to Jerusalem to experience things the West Bank does not necessarily have, like box office movie theaters. It is not allowed to have a West Banker passenger with you in a car with a yellow plate that indicates you are born in Israeli territories, including Jerusalem. Jowana and I would check in the car at the checkpoint, while the other two West Banker friends step out of the car every time and walk to the physical check area.

One time, I wanted to take my friend from Bethlehem to the mall in Jerusalem. There is one checkpoint in the Al-Walaja village where the Israeli soldiers barely stop the car. Throughout the ride, we were hoping they would not stop us because if they did, I would have been documented for carrying a West banker with me. The best-case scenario would be them sending us back.

The last basic human right lacking in Palestine is access to electricity. The West Bank depends on the electricity generated by Israel. According to Susan Power in *Exploiting and Preventing the Development of Oil and Gas in the Occupied Palestinian Territory*, "In 1967, Israel terminated local Palestinian supply agreements for electricity and granted new concessions to the Israel Electric Corporation (IEC) allocating control over the Palestinian electricity grid to the IEC."[33]

Thus, Israel has the right to cut the electricity flowing to the West Bank whenever they chose to, and they do.

To summarize, Palestinians lack basic human rights like having access to water, air, freedom of movement, and electricity. And sadly, many Palestinians are not aware it isn't normal not to have any of them.

---

33 Susan Power, *Annexing Energy: Exploiting and Preventing the Development of Oil and Gas in the Occupied Palestinian Territory* (Ramallah: Al-Haq, 2015, 12.

ORIENTALISM AND POST-COLONIALISM

"You cannot continue to victimize someone else just because you yourself were a victim once—there has to be a limit"[34]

EDWARD SAID

Disclaimer: I will be ruining some of your Disney childhood favorites in this section.

Orientalism is not mentioned here to elaborate on how other Arab women and I are perceived as exotic in the Western world for our looks or accent. I will not use orientalism to critique the people who backlashed Huda Kattan, the founder of Huda Beauty high-end makeup, for creating pastel eyeshadow palettes. They claimed such soft colors do not match her Arabian theme of the desert and gems either. I will use it to mainly analyze the Palestinian context.

Orientalism is a term created by the Palestinian intellectual thinker and theorist Edward Said. I simply define it as racism towards Arabs. *Orientalism* is also a book where Said writes,

> Orientalism can be discussed and analyzed as the corporate institution for dealing with the Orient—dealing with it by making statements about it, authorizing views of it, describing it, by teaching it, settling it, ruling over it: in short, orientalism as a Western-style for dominating restructuring, and having authority over the Orient.[35]

---

34 "A Quote by Edward W. Said," *Goodreads*, accessed October 3, 2020.

35 Edward W. Said, *Orientalism* (London: Routledge and Kegan Paul, 1978), 11.

Even though the Occident contrasts the Orient, and it represents Western power, Said says,

> The Orient...is based on the Orient's special place in European Western experience. The Orient is not only adjacent to Europe; it is also the place of Europe's greatest and richest and oldest colonies, the source of its civilizations and languages, its cultural contestant, and one of its deepest and most recurring images of the other. In addition, the Orient has helped to define Europe (or the West) as its contrasting image, idea, personality, experience.[36]

Those who know what orientalism is would describe it as the superior western discrimination of culture towards the East and its 'inferior' people—the Other. This includes depicting Middle Eastern women as exotic and Arab men as savages. Of course, giving this image to the East would increase the powers and superiority of the West. It started with mainly the imperialism of Britain and France in the Middle East before WWII. Since then, the US takes on this role of power over the Middle East.

As a result of the polarization of power, the perception of Arabs is negative in Hollywood movies. In most cases, Arabs are unaware of this portrayal. I recall how happy I was as a child and a teenager to see my people represented in Western movies. However, I was oblivious to the stereotypical, inaccurate image such movies represented of me as an Arab. To clarify, in such movies, Arabs are the bad guys who kidnap

---

36 Edward W. Said, *Orientalism*, 9–10

the white girl. Later on, this beautiful white woman is saved by the white, macho male figure of the movie like Indiana Jones.

After the 9/11 incident and Osama Bin Laden's al-Qaeda, followed by The Islamic State of Iraq and Levant (ISIL), Arabs would be represented as terrorists in movies. In most cases, there would be one good Arab who chooses to help the Western protagonist. These Arabs balance out all the evilness and terrorism of all the other Arab or Muslim characters.

Looking at Disney's *Aladdin* briefly, Jasmine and Aladdin are the main two characters in the movie, and they have an American accent. Ja'far, the antagonist, and his men, the so-called bad guys, have a strong, aggressive accent, and the depiction of them is evil. They even appear to look ugly. The fact is, the entire movie plays in this orientalist fantasy where characters are either thieves, sultans, sorcerers, genies, belly dancers, or even a man who swallows swords.

The opening song itself describes the fictional Eastern city Agrabah as racist/orientalist as a "barbaric" place.[37] If Arabs did not like the way one looked, they would cut off one's ear. Despite that, it's a place Arabs call "home."[38] A distinguished professor in Islamic Art, Walter Denny, says, "The first three or four minutes of the Disney movie, *Aladdin*, are very prejudicial. They create a very, very, false, and very, very, prejudicial view of the Islamic world."[39]

---

37 "Aladdin," *Disney*, produced by Walt Disney Feature Animation (Burbank, CA: Walt Disney Pictures, 1992), DVD.

38 Ibid.

39 Omar Duwaji, "Why Arabs And Muslims Aren't Exotic," AJ+, December 10, 2017, YouTube video, 9:39.

58 · THE FUTURE OF PALESTINE

This engrains the idea that these people and this place are either dangerous or magical and dreamy—a place described much like Africa in Conrad's *Heart of Darkness*. It is simply wrong!

Going into detail with this is easy but endless, and it is not the point. There is a big chunk of orientalism that discusses post-colonialism.

Orientalism explains the binary relationship between the East and the West. The Orient and the Occident are manmade. Therefore, as much as the West itself, the Orient is an idea that has a history and a tradition of thought, imagery, and vocabulary that have given it reality and presence in and for the West. The two geographical entities thus support and, to an extent, reflect each other.[40]

To apply post-colonialism, a section that falls under orientalism, to the Palestinian context, when Balfour wrote his declaration, he perceived himself as superior for giving a whole land that is not his to another group of people. Edward Said elaborated on that more reading some of Balfour's other letters. If we look at today's situation, Israel functions as the Occident not only to Palestine but to the whole Orient as well. Palestinians buy their water and electricity from Israel, which indicates their inferiority in their own country, but Israel is a child of the West. Look at the West (mostly the US in the twenty-first century) as the father and Israel as the son. The father sends his son to the Middle East to test the waters and perhaps spy, while the son would do anything to please his father. After all, the father gave him what he wanted—a land.

---

40   Edward W. Said, *Orientalism*, 13.

To conclude, orientalism is dangerous and depicts a stereo-typical, prejudicial image of Arabs in general and Palestinians specifically. As for post-colonialism, Israel represents the new Occident in the Middle East when it comes to the notion of power.

TAKEAWAYS

- Every narrative has a protagonist and an antagonist.

- The persecution of the Jews that peaked in WWII in Europe leads them to seek Palestine as their new home and State.

- History shows Palestine has never been free.

- Al-Nakba alone refugeed hundreds of thousands of Palestinians, and Israel confiscated their land in 1967.

- Palestinians' lack of basic human rights, access to water and air, freedom of movement, and access to electricity, are widely normalized.

- Palestinian holders of the blue ID are more privileged than those with the green ID.

- Orientalism is Racism towards Arabs and should be stopped.

- Israel is the new Occident in post-colonial terms.

CHAPTER TWO

THE TRAUMA: INDIVIDUAL AND COLLECTIVE

———

To be a patriotic Palestinian is to put your life in danger.

"Delete your Instagram post on Palestine *right now!*"

"Don't get involved in political parties at your university."

"Why would you write a book on Palestine?"

are typical examples of what I would hear my mom frequently telling me. She would say, "I just don't want them to arrest you. Do you watch the *news*? They just killed a young autistic man."

On May 30, 2020, Iyad Al Hallak was shot twice by two Israeli security soldiers while walking to his special needs school in East Jerusalem. The soldiers anticipated Iyad to be armed, but he was not. His father described him as a "childlike" boy who could not differentiate nationality or religion. They were "all the same for him."[41]

Therefore, I have been living a lie my whole life—not being true to myself; not being able to express my political views; repressing my patriotic and humanitarian drives. As a Jerusalemite with an overprotective mother, loving Palestine seemed taboo to me since it could deprive me of my blue ID.

"Your blue ID is as important as your own being," my mom often says.

Having a blue ID at least guarantees me partial basic rights rather than none. On paper, I am from Israel, and this is what you get for being born in Jerusalem. It has always made my mom happy.

"You should thank your God a thousand times you were born in Jerusalem," she says almost every day.

I am privileged. I am freer than other Palestinians in the West Bank or Gaza in regards to mobility. Yet, it comes with consequences. It took me long enough to realize it is okay to be patriotic despite being shamed by some of my family members for titling my book *The Future of Palestine*, for example. Would it affect my well-being if I were physically politically active? Probably, but it is not about me only. It could affect my family's well-being too, and any mistake can deprive them of their blues IDs, thus, their

---

41   Harry Fawcett, "Anger at Killing of Autistic Palestinian by Israeli Police," *Al Jazeera*, June 2, 2020.

rights. Palestinians can easily be taken to political prisons. Isn't that traumatizing?

The depiction of Palestinians as monsters is traumatizing. Their hunt for a free land is traumatizing. The Israeli Occupation itself is traumatizing. And the trauma is on the personal and communal levels. Combine the shared trauma of constant war and imposition of institutionalized discrimination against Palestinians with one's trauma. The effect is damaging, like a bad chemical reaction. By contrast, Israelis are also traumatized within Israel. I say that not for the sake of sympathy but to spotlight the unspoken within the Israeli community.

THE DEHUMANIZATION OF PALESTINIANS

In front of the eight-meter-high separation wall sits a drab, dystopian themed hotel. All nine rooms look out onto the wall's concrete slabs.[42] If it sounds like the worst hotel view in the world, that is precisely the point. British activist and artist Banksy designed Bethlehem's Walled Off Hotel. Every inch of the space displays Banksy's penchant for playful, political, and poignant protest—nowhere more so than in the hotel's museum.

Banksy's museum seeks to explain the Palestinian struggle through art. In one piece, entitled *Operation 'Protective Edge,'* the artist visualizes the disequilibrium not only between two people's power but also between the value of their lives. The

---

42 Jonathan Cook, "Inside Banksy's The Walled Off Hotel in Bethlehem," (The National, December 22, 2018).

art is of a libra with one human tooth on one side weighing more than two thousand teeth on the other. The side with one tooth represents an Israeli death.

Mathematically speaking, according to statistics displayed alongside the artwork on the 2014 operation Protective Edge on Gaza, the death of one Israeli is worth more than the death of 2000 Palestinians.[43] Noam Chomsky's words spoken at Barnard College in 2011 summarize the situation best: "Israeli Jews are people. Palestinians are unpeople."[44]

Aljazeera, Haaretz, and CNN respectively report, "Palestinian dies after being shot, detained by the Israeli army,"[45] "Palestinian Shot Dead by Israeli Forces,"[46] "Unarmed Palestinian man shot dead by police in Jerusalem."[47] Different Newspapers, but one story repeated over and over again. What I hear is, "It is okay for Palestinians to die every day. Frequent bombings are acceptable for Gaza. It's normal to have peace with Israel." Because of the many stories I hear about Palestinians dying under Israeli bullets and Gazans burnt under Israeli missiles, my emotions slowly turned into unmeltable ice. Other Arab countries, like the United Arab

---

43 David Collier, "Banksy West Bank Bethlehem Hotel Review: An Antisemitic Sham," *The David Collier blog (blog)*, May 10, 2018.

44 "Chomsky on Palestinian Unpeople," *Antony Loewenstein (blog)*, October 19, 2011, accessed September 21, 2020.

45 Al Jazeera, "Israel Admits Holding Body of Palestinian Killed in West Bank," October 9, 2020.

46 Jack Khoury, Yaniv Kubovich, and Hagar Shezaf, "Palestinian Shot Dead by Israeli Forces; Army Says He Threw Firebombs at Soldiers," Haaretz.com, October 5, 2020.

47 Abeer Salman and Andrew Carey, "Unarmed Palestinian Man Shot Dead by Police in Jerusalem," CNN (Cable News Network, May 31, 2020).

Emirates (UAE), have been signing peace treaties with Israel, normalizing horrendous acts against Palestinians. The portrayal of Palestinian rights and lives appears so worthless that even I am starting to believe it. That is how I knew we do not recognize how dangerous it is to dehumanize Palestinians.

Palestinians are not always victims. They did stab a few Israeli Defense Forces (IDF) soldiers. However, why are Palestinians mostly remembered as monsters to the world despite their trauma?

I believe that murder should never be justified. However, kitchen knives are probably not as dangerous as the rifles legally used by the IDF against any Palestinian for self-defense purposes, for example, because we are dangerous. Palestinian stabbing of IDF soldiers and Israeli Policemen was the news's hot topic a few years back. But Palestinians would almost always end up dead by several bullets tearing their bodies apart. In most cases, the Israeli soldiers survived. Here is an example: in August 2020, "a Palestinian stabbed a policeman in the chest in the Old City of Israeli-annexed east Jerusalem. The officer suffered only minor injuries and shot dead his attacker."[48]

In comparison, Israeli soldiers killed several innocent Palestinian civilians because they thought Palestinians armed themselves with knives. Hence, Israeli soldiers would put a knife on the ground for media purposes to demonize Palestinians to the world and victimize themselves.

---

48 The New Arab Staff & Agencies, "Israeli Police Hold Palestinian Man over Knife Killing," *The New Arab*, August 26, 2020.

At the age of fourteen, Sabreen Mujahid Sanad was seen in a video in December 2015 with three IDF soldiers. In the video, the soldiers were trying to arrest her, but she was trying to talk them out of it.

> One of the soldiers throws what appears to be a knife onto the ground. The girl, with her arms raised near her chest, trembles. The soldier then appears to order her to bend down and pick up the knife. She kneels and picks it up, and then appears to talk to the soldier as she holds it. As she kneels, a second soldier aims his weapon at her. A third soldier then approaches and leads her away with her hands behind her back.[49]

If we are asking, "Who started the problem?" we would get stuck in an endless loop. Both sides are in the wrong, and both sides are prejudicial towards each other. This hatred on both sides has so deeply emerged in many of Palestinians and Israelis that our humanity is lost. Thus, despite the normalized Palestinian-Israeli conflict, Palestinians must preserve their humanity.

THE NOTION OF FREEDOM

Despite how the world views us, Palestinians remain humans who lack all types of freedom. On a large scale, the absence of their self-determination rights, for example is caused by an outsider influence: The illegal Israeli occupation. "Israel's settlement policy…violates a special category of obligations

---

49 Ali Abunimah, "Video: Israeli Soldier Forces Knife on Palestinian Girl," *The Electronic Intifada*, December 2, 2015.

entitled peremptory norms of international law (jus cogens) from which no derogation is permitted."[50] That is one of the reasons why Palestinians share a collective trauma.

In an ideal world, freedom is people's decision to do the things they love and enjoy the most without worrying about how expensive their hobbies might be. The global capitalist system makes it impossible for me to travel the world if I do not have the money. If I enjoyed writing, I would have to have the money to publish. If I enjoyed cooking, I would have to worry about getting the ingredients. In most cases, you have to pay to do the things you love. Even if you did not have to pay for it, like singing and dancing, you cannot be doing them for the rest of your life. How would you survive? In this dream world, machines do everything for you. You just have to sit back, relax, and enjoy doing what makes you happy. However, in the real world, freedom is viewed differently and is varied in quantity from one place to another.

When the 2019 novel coronavirus outbreak spread around the globe, people had to stay at home for everyone's safety. A fraction of Americans from the far rightwing fringe of the Republican Party were the first to go on demonstrations. One lockdown protest sign, amongst the many bizarre ones, specifically caught my attention. It said, "Freedom Over Safety."[51]

Different people have different views, and I might not agree with many of these views. The idea of freedom over safety,

---

50   "Chapter 3: Israeli Settlements and International Law," Amnesty International, accessed October 18, 2020.

51   Reuben Salsa, "11 Best COVID-19 Protest Signs," Medium (Better Marketing, April 23, 2020).

especially as a Palestinian, is one with which I highly disagree. Since Palestinians have never had their freedom, they are obsessed with the idea of having it. They are willing to risk their lives because of the desire to have that unattainable freedom. Not that they should, but they do. The price of throwing one small piece of rock is equal to a bullet in the thrower's heart.

"Free Palestine," Palestinians demand.

Embedded in the subconscious of Palestinians is the idea of a free Palestine. Thus, they become rebellious against the things that steal their freedom away. They would react to the outside factors the way they do with the occupation.

In the first couple of months of the coronavirus outbreak, it was easy for Palestinians to stay home. Jamil Khader, a Palestinian thinker and researcher, also my professor, notes that Palestinians handled the outbreak in the winter of 2020 pretty well. He says they are accustomed to responding to disasters.[52] The city of Bethlehem specifically quarantined the first few infected with the virus in a hotel. The municipality locked down every street that leads to the hotel and the city in general.

Even with the second wave in July 2020, both governments in the Holy Land—the Palestinian and Israeli—were strict about their safety regulations. In May, things changed. During the midst of the third month's quarantine of the coronavirus pandemic, the Palestinian government stressed less about the

52   *Victor Diab,* "Victor Diab and Jamil Khader," May 25, 2020, video, 1:03:03.

restrictions. Many Palestinians chose to pretend the virus did not exist saying, "There is no virus. It's all lies!" They believed it is a conspiracy theory of governments against the people. The Palestinian nature of rebellion was dangerous in this context as it sacrificed lives.

I am part of many social Palestinian groups on Facebook (FB). In May 2020, I saw many Palestinians proudly posting their big gatherings that were either religious, like mass prayers, or social, like weddings. In the pictures posted on these FB groups, none of the Palestinians were wearing masks or gloves, nor were they keeping their distance. When the Palestinian government demanded all shops and roads to be locked down, many kept their shops open. The gatherings continued in the following months.

At some point, my cousin was mentioning the looks she got when wearing a mask in public.

A shopkeeper asked my other cousin, "Why are you wearing a mask? Are you worried about your life?"

In September and November 2020, the Holy Land went under a second and a third lockdown because of big gatherings.

COLLECTIVE TRAUMA

Every individual suffers from personal traumas. But Palestinians, similar to the African American community, share a collective trauma because of the Israeli Occupation.

Palestinians, in one way or the other, can relate to each other through their collective trauma. Collective trauma or transgenerational trauma is a trauma that "happens to large groups of people—attempted genocide, war, disease, a terrorist attack. Its effects are specific: fear, rage, depression, survivor guilt, and physical responses in the brain and body that can lead to illness and a sense of disconnection or detachment. Collective trauma can be transmitted down generations and throughout communities."[53]

For Palestinians, the main cause is the Israeli Occupation and the constant, endless war over the land. I am one of those Palestinians who grow up to disconnection and detachment to Palestine. I even defend Palestine from a humanitarian point of view rather than a patriotic one. "In Berkeley, California, Palestinians and Israelis in a workshop circle pass around an invisible object called 'hope'" despite the collective trauma.[54]

Even though it is unlikely on a larger scale, I fear Palestinians will become the oppressors one day. Their unfair life causes them to rage. Thus, we, Palestinians, must heal before we become the monsters that were once the victim. This book is one step closer to our healing. In the least, it prevents the monstrosity we see on a smaller level in the way we deal with others. Does hope really exist?

There is a Palestinian collective trauma. Yet, every person's individual traumas also shape their identity. In fact, according to the psychoanalyst Jacques Lacan, the first shared trauma all humans experience is that of birth "because we all emerge

---

53   Lisa Gale Garrigues and Lisa Gale Garrigues, "Slave and Slaveholder Descendants Break Free of History's Trauma—Together," Yes! Magazine, August 3, 2013.

54   Ibid.

into the same 'Other environment.'"[55] But, traumas keep happening and not only to Palestinians. What about foreigners who end up living in the land for marrying a Palestinian? What about the trauma within Palestine?

SPOUSES OF PALESTINIANS

Olivia is a blonde, short-haired, middle-aged Dutch mom of two. She has a strong Dutch accent and speaks excellent Arabic. She first volunteered in Palestine in 2007 as part of the Olive Harvest Program. She says she had orientalist views initially, like many other volunteers in Palestine due to the media and Hollywood films. Yet, she felt a "strong sense of belonging." She chose to stay and work in Palestine. After a few years, she met a Palestinian man who is now her husband. They both live in Jerusalem.

Olivia admits that she is luckier than other Palestinians' spouses as her husband is a blue ID holder. Unlike her friend, whose husband is a green ID holder, Olivia didn't have to deal with "deeper issues with the Israeli government." Still, the blue ID comes with its consequences in this scenario as well. She says, "I didn't really have a choice on where I wanted to give birth...If I gave birth in the Netherlands, it would be very complicated to get [my children] the Jerusalem ID." Olivia added that because she is not Jewish and her husband is a Palestinian in Jerusalem, they didn't issue her children a birth certificate at first. Therefore, she had to apply for it at the Israeli Ministry of Interior. She describes

---

55   Ali Yansori, "The Concept of Trauma in Lacanian Psychoanalysis," *Psychoanalýza dnes*, December 25, 2018.

it as unwelcoming. "They stalled and stalled and asked [her] for paperwork."

Olivia vividly describes her experience at the Ministry of the Interior as "humiliating." She had to go there at least once a year, especially before getting married, so that she could enter and exit the country. She describes her "awful experience" at the Wadi Al-Joz Ministry of the Interior in Jerusalem: "You stand outside to wait before you can go inside to wait to be searched to go to another place where you wait so you can get a number. By the time it's your turn, you feel like you're a donkey. And I think this is a strategy. The way they deal with you is not a nice way either."

The Tel Aviv Ben-Gurion airport security was another humiliating experience for Olivia. While working in Palestine before meeting her husband, she had to assign a lawyer who could help her travel back and forth between Palestine and the Netherlands. She had to lie about her job and to pretend she was a tour guide. She often denied doing voluntary work, and as speculated, she was interrogated and questioned about her stay in Palestine.

"I don't like it, but you just have to lie," she says.

The hardest part for Olivia was that she could not travel with her newborn to see her parents. Olivia says, "It took me ten months when my daughter was already sitting up straight, started to say her first words, and wasn't this baby anymore before we could finally travel. So, that was difficult."

When I first met Olivia for the interview, she said she had to ask about me before agreeing to the interview. The name,

Tamar, could be of an Israeli. Tamar is a name mentioned in the Torah and the Old Testament. Olivia told me, "If you were Israeli, I wouldn't want you to interview me." After hearing her story, it made more sense to me. She could risk everything, which is why I had to change her real name and call her Olivia.

I do respect the fact that she still managed to choose to live in Palestine. She went through processes and paperwork she wouldn't have to go through if she married someone from the Netherlands. I reckon it is brave of her, even for choosing to live the Palestinian life with all its checkpoints, walls, and limitations. She does not have to go through it, but she did. She did emphasize every day. Lastly, she admitted she was privileged first coming to Palestine, and like many other volunteers, enjoyed helping Palestinians. However, now, she shares the same trauma with every Palestinian, and not many can do that.

ISRAELI TRAUMA

Many Palestinians are unaware of the problems within Israel. Anna Kleiman depicts the unspoken brutality within Israel. On a systemic level, discrimination against Israeli citizens is one problem, and on a personal level, mental health is another one.

Anna Kleiman is a young feminist and LGBT activist who was born in Russia. She has been an Israeli citizen since the age of two. She has green and blue hair and a few fairly small tattoos here and there. Her biggest tattoo is an eagle with spread wings on her calf. She rides a motorcycle with a black leather jacket and shorts. I first met Anna in the summer of 2017 at Georgetown University as part of the Middle East Partnership Initiative Student Leaders program (MEPI-SLP). She wasn't accepted by the students of the MENA region (the Middle East and North Africa) for her Israeli nationality. Yet, she was strong enough to deal with their judgment. Let's face it, we didn't all start as great leaders.

After the fall of the Union of Soviet Socialist Republics (USSR) in 1990, most of Russia was hit with poverty. Anna says, "We were four people in my family, two parents, my sister and me, and we got to a really dark place, sharing an apple for dinner." Due to her father's Zionist views and her mother's "survival and economic" views, they decided to move to Israel. Anna explains, "My mom is Christian, and my father's father was Jewish. This means our family was eligible to receive citizenship in Israel, which was 'calling' Jews from all over the world to immigrate to Israel."

In Hebrew schools, like most Israeli school kids, Anna did not learn much about the Palestinian narrative that is sealed and buried away from the eyes of Israeli citizens nowadays. She claims that "information on the occupation and what it actually looks like [was] not coming through. Now I can look back and say that me, like all others, we're brainwashed, believing it's better if I would be that soldier on the border than some right-wing violent sh*t-head." She then continued by adding that the segregation between Israelis and Palestinians is strong, and it is part of Israel's plan. Furthermore, it was hard for her to find information on what is happening in Palestine. She claims, "Nowhere in Hebrew can I find news on what is happening in the West Bank, Gaza, or East

Jerusalem. I started understanding I have to follow British, American, different Arab news and opinion leaders, and Instagram pages to be able to hear what the government is putting so much effort into hiding."

Even though Anna is considered Israeli, she, like Palestinians, is also considered a second-class citizen in Israel. Anna mentions that because "Judaism is passed by the mother," Anna and her family are not considered Jewish by the religious laws in Israel. She elaborates, "None of us have full rights. My sister and I have no legal religion. Because in Israel, marriage is allowed only within one's religion, all social benefits that follow marriage, like discounts on apartments and different bills, etc., we don't have." As a consequence, Anna deduces that she, like many Russian women, "the enemies of the country" are "targeted for military or state conversion to Judaism." She goes further to question conservative Israeli politicians who assume "Russian women are worse than Arabs." They are a threat because they "give birth to non-Jewish babies."

Today, Anna votes for the Palestinian party during the elections. Personally, as an Arab Jerusalemite with a Jordanian passport, I can't even vote. She is also disgusted by the fact she "pay[s] taxes that go straight to torturing and oppressing other people in a fascist way, not very different from the Nazis."

Despite all of her political struggles, Anna admits she is more privileged than Palestinians. Yet, on an individual level, Anna suffers from trauma and receives therapy. She was raped by "a guy in [her] school, [her] age," and she blames it on her abusive dad.

Anna didn't have a decent father figure in her life. She illustrates him as a "violent, racist, homophobic piece of sh*t, woman hater as well as a chronic liar." Her mother, whom Anna calls "the slayer queen," kicked him out when Anna was fifteen years old. Her father punished her "for completely random things: losing stuff, breaking stuff, hurting [herself] by accident, smiling too much, arguing, insisting, proving him wrong." One time at the age of twelve, she became so scared for speaking back to him that she hurt herself with the not so sharp knife she was using to crack nuts. She hid her wounded hand under the table. She kept eating the nuts, so he didn't notice and bled for over twenty minutes. When her mother got back home, she immediately noticed Anna's pale face.

As a result, Anna "learned to freeze and not to take attention from a very young age, anything could be a reason for [her] punishment. [she] learned [she is] actually worthless, everything [she] touched becomes garbage." She says that at seventeen, "I was raped. I froze and couldn't move just like I used to freeze in the living room to avoid being targeted by my father."

Anna refused to change the last name she got from her father. She justifies, "I am reclaiming my last name. He would want it to be associated with his hatred and disgust, but no one will remember his narrow views on the world. Looking for a Kleiman, you'll find inclusive feminism, anti-capitalism, and anti-racism."

Anna does not share our Palestinian collective trauma, but one cannot neglect that living in this country comes with consequences for both sides. Plus, every person's individual trauma makes it worse.

THE OLYMPICS OF VICTIMIZATION

There is no doubt that what happens to Palestinians today is inhumane and unacceptable. However, Palestinians don't need to start a race of who is victimized the most. It does not and would not get them anywhere.

When it comes to Israel's religious argument, a fun fact is, the majority of Jews worldwide consider themselves nonreligious. According to the poll *The Global Index of Religion and Atheism of 2012* conducted by Gallup on 51,927 people of fifty-seven different countries,

> Of the religions surveyed in the poll, Jews were found to be the least religious: Only thirty-eight percent of the Jewish population worldwide considers itself religious, while fifty-four sees itself as nonreligious, and two percent categorize themselves as atheists. In comparison, ninety-seven percent of Buddhists, eighty-three percent of Protestant Christians, and seventy-four percent of Muslims consider themselves religious.[56]

For one to believe, somebody else has to believe for them. In the case of Israel, Christian Zionists, and Muslim Zionists, like Saudi Arabia, believed in Israel. They believed God gave Palestine to the Jewish people. The statistics above show that the being of Israel is not about a religious argument anymore if it were for people's religious beliefs. After all, that religious belief of God's chosen people eventually leads to the collective

---

56 "New Poll Shows Atheism on Rise, with Jews Found to Be Least Religious," *Haaretz*, January 11, 2018.

trauma of Palestinians through wars and their deprivation of basic human rights.

Everyone struggles and every person is traumatized in a way or another. Individually, collectively, or both. Jamil Khader critiques Palestinians' pursue of victimization writing, "Many a time, members of oppressed communities end up engaged in an Olympics for victimization, in which they deem their struggle as more important than the struggle of other groups."[57] This does not lead Palestinians anywhere.

In psychoanalytical terms, as humans, we want to fulfill our desires. Each claiming the land as theirs is a form of trying to attain an unattainable desire, and such individual ideologies make us happy. Our traumas lead us to be overprotective about what belongs to us in an unhealthy, dangerous manner. This is when our obsession with having a perfect, inclusive, fulfilling identity comes into play.

TAKEAWAYS

- Palestinians are dehumanized.

- Illegal modern-day colonization of Israel is normalized.

- Freedom is essential, but the obsession over it is problematic.

---

57 Jamil Khader, "Architectural Parallax, Neoliberal Politics and the Universality of the Palestinian Struggle: Banksy's Walled Off Hotel," *European Journal of Cultural Studies* 23, no. 3 (2020): pp. 485.

- Palestinians share the collective trauma of the occupation in addition to their own traumas.

- Foreigners living in Palestine automatically become part of the Palestinian collective trauma.

- Many suffer from trauma, including Israelis, on a systemic and individual level.

- The religious argument of Israel leads to Palestinian trauma despite being invalid today.

- An Olympics of victimization does not get an oppressed nation anywhere.

CHAPTER THREE

THE DISCOURSE ON IDENTITY: IS IT IMPORTANT OR NOT?

———

"For a people without a land, a land without a people."[58]

It is that time when Jewish people did not have a land.

It us the time when Palestine does not have its people.

That is when the clash of civilization begins, and a useless, infinite loop is created.

THE PALESTINIAN IDENTITY

Defining identity, "identity encompasses the memories, experiences, relationships, and values that create one's sense of

---

58   Adam M Garfinkle, "On the Origin, Meaning, Use and Abuse of a Phrase," Middle Eastern Studies 27, no. 4 (1991): 539. Accessed September 30, 2020.

self."[59] The concept of identity is controversial. Scholars like Amin Maalouf argue that studying identity is essential in depicting the negative effects of Western colonization of the Middle East. Others, like the philosopher, Slavoj Žižek, chose to focus on concrete universality in a capitalist world based on reconfiguring identity and linking the struggles of different people to solidarity politics.[60] A concrete universal is, "a universal whose connotation is so particularized that it denotes one concrete reality especially an organized unity as distinguished from a universal that denotes any one of a class—used by Hegelians to contrast terms such as *man, book,* or *church* with those that denote a totality, as *mankind, literature, the church*"[61] One's identity is important, but considering culture an affiliation to identity is problematic because it discriminates and divides people.

In his book, *In the Name of Identity: Violence and the Need to Belong*, Maalouf writes, "We cannot be satisfied with forcing billions of bewildered human beings to choose between the excessive assertion of their identity and the loss of their identity altogether, between fundamentalism and disintegration."[62] "Identity can't be compartmentalized," he argues. "You can't divide it up into halves or thirds or any other separate segments. I haven't got several identities: I've got just one, made

---

59 Psychology Today, "Identity," accessed October 6, 2020.

60 Hatem Bazian, "Dr. Hatem Bazian Conversation with Professor Jamil Khader, Dean of Research at Bethlehem University," October 3, 2020, video, 1:22:56.

61 Merriam Webster, s.v. "Concrete Universal," accessed October 5, 2020.

62 Amin Maalouf, *In the Name of identity: Violence and the Need to Belong,* trans. Barbara Bray (New York: Penguin books, 2000), 35.

up of many components in a mixture that is unique to me, just as other people's identity is unique to them as individuals."[63]

Every day, the Palestinian identity comes into question so much that I wonder, *Will we still hear the word Palestine a hundred years from now?* Some world powers are eliminating the name Palestine from the map. On May 14, 2018, US President Donald Trump carried out his plans to relocate the US Embassy from Tel Aviv to Jerusalem. And just like that, Israel's long-disputed claim to Jerusalem—my Jerusalem—as its capital city had the official blessing of the United States of America. Inside the US Embassy's temporary location that day, hundreds of dignitaries gathered for an opening ceremony. Meanwhile, just miles away at the Gaza border, Palestinian protestors clung to their identity, demanding the right of return to territory that has become part of Israel. In stark contrast to the regal ceremony taking place in the US embassy at that very moment, along the Gaza border, Israeli soldiers unceremoniously shot and killed at least sixty Palestinian protestors.

I still remember Yasser Arafat's declaration of independence of the State of Palestine of 1988 that is played every year on November 15th. His voice rings in my ears, "In the name of God and in the name of the Palestinian Arab people, the National Council declares the creation of the State of Palestine on our Palestinian land with noble Jerusalem as its capital."[64] However, our clinging to this type of idea is toxic since it is a

---

63 Maalouf, *In the Name of Identity*, 2.

64 Ali Salam, "31 Years Ago, Arafat Declared Independence of the State of Palestine," *IMEMC News,* November 14, 2019.

fundamental fantasy. Even though many dismiss the identity of the inhomogeneous Palestinian groups, culture should not be part of that identity.

CULTURE AND FUNDAMENTAL FANTASIES

According to Jacques Lacan, a fundamental fantasy is what happened at castration in terms of possession and loss. "This fantasy thus consoles the subject by positing that s/he at one point did have the phallic Thing, but that then, at castration, it was taken away from him/her by the Other."[65]

Culture is a fundamental fantasy, and this applies to Palestinians. They psychologically believe in the fundamental fantasy of possessing a land and a culture when they don't. They are traumatized by the idea of having a land and a culture and suddenly losing them. According to Zizek's take on fundamental fantasies, "fantasy provides the idea of a privileged object that desire fixates on in order to provide the subject with its relation to it."[66] Therefore, if you have the land, you are privileged. If you have the culture, you have the power. Israel is stealing and appropriating that culture, but Palestinians should understand the importance of universality that transcends them.

As a Palestinian, I dislike seeing huge signs on the wall of Jerusalem with titles like "Israeli foods" with hummus, falafel, and Arabian salad under these titles. Now, the world

---

65 *Internet Encyclopedia of Philosophy*, s.v. "Jacques Lacan," accessed October 5, 2020.

66 *No Subject—Encyclopedia of Psychoanalysis*. s.v. "Fantasy." May 24, 2019.

calls it Israeli salad, and this is the definition of cultural appropriation. The special section for my food labeled as "Israeli falafel" and "Israeli couscous" in my school's cafeteria in the US irritates me. I have known such foods to be Arabian salads and Moroccan or North African couscous. My school and many other institutions in the US should not fall for Israeli propaganda. However, if humans do not claim a certain food, dress, music, art, dance, and so on as theirs, globalization would not really rob us of cultural identity because culture should not be part of identity in the first place.

We live in a universal world. We must not focus on the names and the labels we give to certain things which is what Slavoj Žižek calls concrete universality. His point is that "'concrete universality' means that there is no abstract universality of rules, there are no 'typical' situations, all we are dealing with is exceptions; however, a concrete totality is the totality that regulates the concrete context of exceptions. We should thus, on account of our very fidelity to concrete analysis, reject any form of nominalism."[67]

In simplistic terms, labeling hummus and falafel as either Palestinian, Arab, or Israeli should cease as it contradicts concrete universality that "constitutes the grounds for rethinking identity politics."[68] It creates more feuds on less important issues. Khader explains,

---

67 Jamil Khader, "Architectural Parallax, Neoliberal Politics and the Universality of the Palestinian Struggle: Banksy's Walled Off Hotel," *European Journal of Cultural Studies* 23, no. 3 (2020): pp. 474-494.

68 Khader, "Architectural Parallax, Neoliberal Politics and the Universality of the Palestinian Struggle," 480.

The human subject will never succeed either in using any particular content to fill this universality or in bringing the particular content into harmonious relations with the universal because there is a fundamental contradiction between its 'singular subjective viewpoint', through which it perceives and colors reality, and its status as another object in that reality.[69]

My Tanzanian friend, Naomi, questions cultural appropriation and says, "You can't own culture...Culture spreads, and that's the beauty of it." Culture should be a universal language that is shared and appreciated. It should not give anyone power. It is supposed to connect rather than divide. For example, Naomi loves sharing her African braids and the clothes she makes out of East African fabric with a modern undertaking. However, she understands that in the US, the collective trauma of slavery makes it unacceptable for African Americans to share their culture, especially with their persecutors.

Naomi shared a picture in an African kimono she had made. "This is offensive to Japanese culture," says one of her Instagram friends whose fiancé is Japanese. "Please delete the picture because a kimono is not African," she continues. What this woman didn't understand is that kimonos are also part of the African culture.

Naomi complained to me, "I had to explain to her kimonos are worn in East Africa too."

---

69 Ibid.

On the Palestinian level, our shared trauma forces us to believe we have to cling to a culture. While in California, I had dinner with two Armenian sisters. "I would like to get hummus, please," says Emily, one of the sisters. "I like to stick to what I know." Armenian food is similar to Arabian food: dolma, spicy harissa, pastirma, baklava. The Ottomans had an influence and introduced some of these foods. Thus, culture cannot be claimed because it does not belong to one nation only.

Culture does not define us. Culture should be a universal language. It should not be something we fight over. Then, we can focus on our humanity, especially as dehumanized Palestinians.

THE QUESTIONING OF PALESTINIAN IDENTITY

Being Palestinian is peculiar. How do you introduce yourself as someone from a country that is slowly fading away, a country known around the world by another name?

People often ask me where I am from when I travel abroad. In the past, I offered a simple answer. "I'm from Palestine."

"Pakistan?"

That was the most common reaction. But others I met reacted differently and in a manner that probably said more about them than about my country.

"Oh, you're from Israel!" they would say excitedly. "I've actually been to Israel! Such a beautiful place."

Their words smothered and insulted me. To eradicate such an important element of identity and replace it with another that has nothing to do with me is to question who I am.

I know exactly who I am. But in an attempt to ease these uncomfortable encounters with strangers, I began to alter my answer.

"Where are you from?"

My revised reply: "I am from Jerusalem." I felt like I was selling out, and yet the strangers' response remained the same.

"I've actually been to Israel! Such a beautiful place!"

I used to justify myself at first because each time, I wished I could prove to them Palestine is not a myth. It exists. I wished I could tell them to stop fabricating the story.

The point is, I disappoint them every time.

No, I do not speak Hebrew. No, I am not Jewish. No, I am not from Israel. However, I would explain to them what Palestine is. It was a chance for me to speak up about my history. The response, most of the time, is not a pleasant one.

In 2018 at Hub101, a co-working space and facility of California Lutheran University (CLU), I was responsible for making key cards for customers. One of the customers had the last name "Israel." Because of my accent, she asked me,

"Where are you from?"

"Jerusalem."

"I'm from Israel, too!" she said merrily.

"I'm from Jerusalem, Palestine though," I said.

She boiled with rage.

"You Palestinians celebrate and dance when an Israeli soldier dies," she snapped.

"What do you mean?" I asked, taken aback by her accusation.

"Yes! I've seen it in videos! You love it when we die!"

"But—"

She interrupted me. "You keep stabbing us too whenever you have the chance. You—" She kept going nonstop. I smiled at her face.

"We—"

"I've seen it! It's all on videos. You—" She continued to argue. It was that moment I realized she was not going to allow me to speak.

"Yeah," I nodded instead.

"Anyways, it was good talking to you. I really hope we all get peace one day."

The corners of my glued mouth rose. I was happy to watch her leave.

Nowadays, I say, "I am from Jerusalem, Palestine." Israeli Prime Minister Benjamin Netanyahu may disagree. US President Donald J. Trump may disagree. Ms. Israel herself may even disagree. History, however, is on my side.

REFUGEES AND THEIR DESCENDANTS

When it comes to refugees, Al-Nakba (1948) and Al-Naksa (1967) wars resulted in a few million refugees, as explained earlier. Specifically, "five million Palestine refugees are eligible for UNRWA services."[70] Moreover, "Nearly one-third of the registered Palestine refugees, more than 1.5 million individuals, live in fifty-eight recognized Palestine refugee camps in Jordan, Lebanon, the Syrian Arab Republic, the Gaza Strip and the West Bank, including East Jerusalem."[71]

"More than two million Palestinian refugees are registered with The United Nations Relief and Works Agency (UNRWA). Unlike any other host country, Jordan granted Palestinian refugees full citizenship rights, except for 120,000 people who originally came from the Gaza Strip. There are ten official and three unofficial refugee camps in Jordan."[72] This represents the numbers in Jordan only. So, what are refugee camps exactly?

Palestinian refugee camps are polluted, dull areas in mainly the Levant. Those who were in Syria were refuged again

---

70   "Palestine Refugees," UNRWA, accessed September 22, 2020.

71   Ibid.

72   "Palestine Refugees: Locations and Numbers," The New Humanitarian, January 17, 2018, accessed September 22, 2020.

because of the Syrian civil war (2011–present). These refugee camps started with tents, and some have existed for over fifty-five years.[73] Now, they are simply areas where dignified people cannot live. The buildings are shabby and might fall at any moment. The infrastructure is in poor condition. Water and electricity are barely accessible. Human beings do not deserve that, and the world should be aware of this. But, what about the descendants of those refugees?

* * *

Those five million Palestinian refugees are mostly the descendants of the 1948 and 1967 wars refugees. Hence, these people are Palestinian by blood, as one might say, but most of them have not grown up in or visited Palestine. Amjaad is an example of a descendant of Palestinian refugees who has never been to Palestine.

Amjaad is a Jordanian woman born to Palestinian parents. She is a close friend of mine whom I met at Georgetown University in Washington, DC, as part of the Middle East Partnership Initiative Student Leaders Program (MEPI-SLP). She is the definition of short and cute. The shape of her brown eyes is similar to a cat's. Long, dark, straight hair sits alongside her full lips. When I first met her, she covered her hair, but she doesn't anymore because it was her mother's wish to wear hijab rather than hers.

When Amjaad first knew I was from Jerusalem, Palestine, it was her instinct to approach me. She did. She saw a missing

---

73   Ron Wilkinson, "Where Are the Tents? It Is a Camp, Isn't It?" *BADIL Resource Center for Palestinian Residency and Refugee Rights*, accessed September 22, 2020.

element of her identity in me, and I have recently decided to ask her about it.

"My dad was born in Palestine, in Hebron, in 1954." She tells me, "my [paternal] grandparents were told that they must leave the country for a few days in 1967, but they were never allowed to go back again." When I asked her about it, she added that Palestinians chose to protect their families from the war, for it was an easy victory for Israel against surrounding Arab countries.

"Massacres were committed in areas like Der Yasmin and other areas near Hebron," Amjaad says. She also mentions that Jordan was the "closest option" that protected them from the cruelty of the IDF soldiers. As for her mother, it's a different story. She says, "My mother's father came to work in Jordan around 1950 and stayed there. The war prevented him from visiting his country as he used to before with his wife and kids."

To Amjaad, there has always been something missing. She says, "I used to be confused when I was a kid. We love the country we live in, but we simply don't belong here." She also describes how sad she is for not being able to visit her true homeland yet. It would be a long, complicated process too. She mentions how she would have to apply for a visa. It is more complicated for her as she has relatives in Palestine.

"I am very proud of my identity, and I enjoy listening to the stories I hear about what my grandparents went through, and I take that as part of my identity as well," Amjaad says. She accepts her reality as a descendant of Palestinian refugees, but it's not that easy in Jordan or even other parts of the Arab world.

In Jordan, for example, where the tribal system still exists, Palestinians are very likely to face discrimination. Amjaad says that usually, Palestinians in Jordan are proud to say they are Palestinian. However, one time, she was in a very uncomfortable situation pretending she belonged to one of the big Jordanian tribes.

There is also institutional discrimination. "Some business owners actually ask about your nationality," she says. For example, Amjaad's mother saw a job posting for a library and thought it was a good idea for Amjaad to start working there. Amjaad says, "[My mom] asked them about it so I can apply. The employer first asked where I was from."

"From Hebron," Amjaad's mother answered.

"Well, actually, we don't need any employees now," the employer said.

Moreover, there is even discrimination in marriage. According to Amjaad, if the wife is Palestinian and the husband is Jordanian, the wife will be looked down upon for not having pure Jordanian blood.

And things keep getting worse and worse with time. To Amjaad, this horrible situation reached its peak when her father died only a month before I interviewed her. Her father was her primary source of those Palestinian stories that she enjoyed hearing—the good, the bad, and the ugly. Despite that, these stories were her only connection to an important aspect of her identity. It disappeared, much like Palestine is currently disappearing.

Amin Maalouf argues, "My identity is what prevents me from being identical to anybody else."[74] Amjaad can believe that she is different from Jordanians as she has Palestinian blood in her, for example. Maalouf adds, "Every one of my allegiances links me to a large number of people. But the more ties I have, the rarer and more particular my own identity becomes."[75] Based on this, Amjaad having Palestinian roots supposedly makes her identity more unique. However, is having a rare identity a good thing when that allegiance leads to her marginalization in Jordan? A deeper and more important question would be, is focusing on our identities even of any importance, and why do we consider it important? Based on concrete universality, the answer is no.

UNDER WHICH PALESTINIAN LABEL ARE YOU?

I wanted to know if 1948 Arabs are more privileged than other Palestinians. To clarify, Palestinians are not a homogenous group of people. There are many types of Palestinians within Palestine. Without considering refugees and immigrants outside Palestine, there are Palestinians in the Gaza Strip who live in an open-air prison because of the restrictions Israel enforces. Just like Palestinians in the West Bank, they both have the green ID and the Palestinian passport, but Gazans are forbidden access to visit other Palestinian territories.

---

74   Amin Maalouf, *In the Name of Identity*, 10.

75   Amin Maalouf, *In the Name of Identity*, 18.

Then, there is Jerusalem. In East Jerusalem, Palestinians have a Jordanian passport. However, they can apply for an Israeli passport. Last but not least, 1948 Palestinians are those who stayed in Palestine during Al-Nakba (1948) despite the war. They live in the Israeli areas today.

I am a Jerusalemite, and my blue ID allows me to travel from Ben-Gurion's airport in Tel Aviv. One time, I had to travel from Jordan just like West Bankers or Gazans (if they could get their permission to go to Jerusalem for their visa interview). As mentioned earlier, I was a participant in the MEPI Student Leaders Program assigned to Georgetown University (GU) in 2017. I was so excited to travel that I had everything already packed more than a month before my flight. All of a sudden, I received an email from the program saying,

> Dear Tamar,
>
> Do you think you can travel from Queen Alia International Airport in Amman, Jordan, with the other Palestinian and Jordanian students?
>
> Best,
> GU SLP

I was willing to do anything for this opportunity. "Yes! I absolutely can." I hastily answered, and I wish I hadn't.

Sheikh Hussein Bridge (Al-Jiser) that connects Palestine to Jordan closes early in the afternoon, and my flight to Washington, DC, was late that night. I woke up early in the morning, crossed the bridge before its closing hour, and waited for eight hours at the Queen Alia International Airport without even checking in. There was no food, and I was by myself. The other students I was traveling with, whom I didn't know then, had family and friends in Jordan. They had spent their evening with their people before coming to the airport.

Fortunately for me, the flight was at night. Had it been a morning flight, I would have had to fork out the money for hotel accommodations for the night, which is what happens in most cases. That was something that showed me how privileged I am to be able to skip these procedures and travel like a normal person. Yes, I am humiliated, stripped naked, and checked physically every time by the Israeli security at the airport, but at least I do not waste a lot of time and money. What do the 1948 Arabs think?

* * *

Privilege depends on demography in Palestine and Israel. I have conducted a miniature research project, surveying 1948 Arabs, Palestinians who live in Israeli areas, about their privileges if they existed. Of the thirty millennial 1948 Arabs who responded to my Facebook questionnaire, most reported they are at both an advantage and a disadvantage.

On the one hand, having Israeli documents and living in Israel as Palestinians come with perks. Most of the interviewees mentioned they are privileged for having the Israeli passport mobility-wise. Being an Israeli on paper, despite the Palestinian nationality, allows 1948 Arabs to travel internationally from the Ben-Gurion Airport in Tel Aviv or the Ramon Airport in Eilat. It also allows them to travel to more countries without a visa and in an easier manner compared to the Jordanian passport.

"I don't want to apply for a visa every time I travel to a country in Europe," one of the interviewees explains.

Others said they are more privileged than other Palestinians for having excellent health and life insurance and a health-care system in general. When it comes to pharmaceuticals in the Palestinian health care system, "drugs are exceptionally expensive. Israeli restrictions on the pharmaceutical market have limited potential for competition to reduce prices."[76] Lastly, some 1948 Arabs believe they are more privileged for a system that allows them to handle some documents online rather than having to stand in line for the whole day for document procedures. Unlike in Israel, even credit card use is rare in Palestine.

On the other hand, living in Israel has its consequences. Many 1948 Palestinians in the survey mention how they are humiliated and discriminated against every day for being of a different religion and language. For example, one of the people surveyed sarcastically said, "Any day, you walk down the street with [Israelis], speaking Arabic, and you barely see any of them giving you dirty looks." 1948 Arabs ought to be able to speak their language in the Israeli parts freely. If I am being honest, even I fear speaking Arabic in the presence of Israelis, maybe to prevent some looks, maybe to avoid discrimination.

---

76 Michaela V. Pfeiffer, *Vulnerability and the International Health Response in the West Bank and Gaza Strip: an Analysis of Health and the Health Sector* (Jerusalem: World Health Organization, 2001).

Another millennial mentions how in his school in Haifa, he does not feel he is the target of discrimination. However, his friends who go to the Hebrew University in Jerusalem mention the amount of hatred they receive on a daily basis verbally or through looks. Palestinians who go to the Hebrew University barely make it. They end up dropping out because they do not feel emotionally and psychologically safe in an environment charged with prejudice. Thus, in most cases, they change schools. Five of my high school classmates were enrolled in the Hebrew University after graduation. Only one of them graduated. The remaining four dropped out after their first year and went to other schools. Moreover, in Hebrew University, for example, Palestinians with a non-Israeli passport are also considered international students. In other words, their tuition is much more than Israeli students.

To conclude, the amount of discrimination towards a Palestinian depends on the geographical region they live in and their governmental identification. They are all unprivileged and considered second class citizens, yet it varies demographically.

TAKEAWAYS

- Culture should not be considered part of identity because it creates fundamental fantasies.

- Names that refer to cultural aspects of a nation or a country should be removed.

- Universality is required to dismiss some of our biases.

- Identifying one's self as Palestinian can be negatively perceived.

- There are five million Palestinian refugees in the world.

- Descendants of Palestinian refugees are marginalized.

- Within Palestine, some Palestinians are more privileged than others depending on their demographical.

PART II

THE DISCRIMINATION WITHIN PALESTINE

CHAPTER FOUR

WHY RELIGION AND NATIONALISM GO HAND IN HAND, UNPLEASANTLY

———

"Do you know who the original Jews are?" a Palestinian-American Uber driver challenges me and my Syrian friend on our way back to the campus.

"Ashkenazi Jews?" I answer confidently.

"Wrong! We are! Palestinian Jews, but we aren't accepted by other Palestinians because of our religion. So, we've been hiding, and that's why you never hear of us."

* * *

Shark-Horse Hybrid (Shorce): A mythical, photoshopped creature, depicted with a shark's head on a horse's body. My

Theoretical Criticism professor, Dr. Jamil Khader, coined the term "Shorce." Pictures of hybrid animals went viral on social media a few years ago as a meme. The internet has articles on the creepiest combinations.

What's shocking is not this virtually created monster that walks on land and has gills. What's shocking is the comments beneath such images on social media. Some Palestinians and Arabs reposted the Shorce on Facebook (FB), saying, "Subhanallah," glorifying Allah's (God's) creation. Not only that, but the number of FB likes such a picture gets is mind-blowing. And those who press the like button believe the Shorce is real. This is why logic must overlap with religion.

Mythical stories catch traction on the internet because humankind has an innate need to believe in something bigger than us, bigger than our comprehension. Dr. Khader criticizes Arabs who believe in everything they see on the internet. He questions our belief and conviction in conspiracy theories. He says that one of the reasons why humans easily believe in anything is because of the claim, "This can't be all there is."[77] This argument is often used in conspiracy theories videos, and it's religious in its core, according to Dr. Khader. Therefore, people should not blindly believe in everything they see or read, especially on unscientific social platforms today.

All extremes are problematic. Extreme, blind religious beliefs slow down our Palestinian civilization, and the nationalistic approach to life can inflict prejudice. Instead, all affiliations, including the religious ones, ought to be tolerated as long as

---

77 *Victor Diab,* "Victor Diab and Jamil Khader," May 25, 2020, video, 1:03:03.

they don't harm anyone. Understanding the historical and cultural gap of our Holy Books helps us overcome bias.

NATIONALISM

Nationalism can be one of the main factors that turn religion into a toxic belief. Religion should focus on love and kindness.

Arab countries and other nations colonized by Western powers can form anti-colonialism as a form of resistance. According to the discourse of anti-colonialists, nationalism developed when "the form of the modern European nation-state was taken over and employed as a sign of resistance."[78] The term explains two phenomena. First, "the attitude that the members of a nation have when they care about their national identity." This phenomena questions national identity usually related to a common origin, cultural ties, or ethnicity, and whether a person's being in a nation ought to be regarded as voluntary or nonvoluntary.[79] Second, "the actions that the members of a nation take when seeking to achieve (or sustain) self-determination." This interrogates self-determination and people's "authority over domestic and international affairs."[80]

Under international law, the right to self-determination is the first and most important right listed. It is the right to determine

---

78 Bill Ashcroft, Gareth Griffiths, and Helen Tiffin, *Post-Colonial Studies: The Key Concepts* (London: Routledge, 2007), 11.

79 *Stanford Encyclopedia of Philosophy*, s.v. "Nationalism," accessed September 21, 2020.

80 Ibid.

people's destiny.[81] Because Palestinians cannot choose their political status, they cannot determine economic, cultural, and social development. How do Palestinians seek to achieve nationalism when they are under occupation? It is impossible.

When a nation is not able to achieve its self-determination, it looks back at times when it was great. The Islamic nation in Palestine may look to the fifth and sixth century for its greatness and find it in the early Islamic conquests that extended the Arabian Empire. One of the most vibrant and powerful empires was that of the Arab world, "which from the founding of the Islamic religion around 610 by Muhammad (ca. 570–632) rapidly expanded to conquer a vast territory from modern-day Pakistan through the Middle East, North Africa, and Spain."[82]

When thinking of the most powerful countries today, none of the Arab countries make it to the top five. Some are more advanced than others, but Palestine remains a nonmember observer state, as stated in the United Nations General Assembly resolution 67/19 on November 29, 2012.[83] But does that mean we should put history on replay, especially when some incidents in history were corruptive? Do we keep making the same mistakes?

The idea here is that nationalism shouldn't slow us down. We had better not look back at the past but rather look forward to

81   "Self-Determination," UNPO, accessed September 22, 2020.

82   James Peter. Burkholder, Donald Jay Grout, and Claude Victor. Palisca, *A History of Western Music* (New York: W.W. Norton and Company, 2019), 63.

83   "A/RES/67/19 of December 4, 2012," *United Nations*, accessed September 22, 2020.

a welcoming, unbiased future. Religion focuses on love. If we don't understand that, it can be toxic, like toxic nationalism that can lead to marginalizing people of different religion, gender, race, or sexual orientation.

THE HISTORICAL AND CULTURAL GAP

Many argue that religion and science cannot overlap, but science doesn't have to contradict religion. The Holy Books, the Torah, the Bible, and the Quran, were written in a time when science, technology, and archeology weren't as advanced as today. People—both religious and nonreligious—are often unaware of the importance of reading these books through the historical and cultural lens. Historical differences of the Holy Books concern technological advances, scientific discoveries like evolution, cosmology, et cetera. In comparison, cultural differences study the food people ate then, the language they spoke, the customs they had, and the social roles they played. How are the two lenses different?

Those who subscribe to a literal interpretation of their Holy Books often hold the text to be infallible. On the one hand, one must understand the historical difference between then and now. Some argue that according to the Bible, the Earth is approximately six thousand years even when scientifically it's about 4.5 billion years.[84] The latter was officially published in 1956 by Claire Patterson in "Age of Meteorites and the Earth."[85] At the time of Biblical writings, mankind didn't have resources to prove the

---

84   Bodie Hodge, "How Old Is the Earth?" Answers in Genesis, May 30, 2007.

85   Claire Patterson, "Age of Meteorites and the Earth," *Geochimica Et Cosmochimica Acta* 10, no. 4 (1956): 230–237.

real age of the Earth. This is what's referred to as a historical gap. Hence, it's essential to tolerate those who believe and those who don't. Some people are logical. They need science to understand life. Others are spiritual, and religion fulfills an important element in their lives. Others are philosophical, and the list goes on. We shouldn't be biased because we are different by nature.

On the other hand, today's cultures stand in stark contrast to the ancient cultures depicted in the Holy Books. These traditions and customs differ geographically from one place to another, and they can be subject to change throughout the ages. Applying the customs and traditions of that period is something some might consider the best way to seek their nationalism. Of course, many customs and traditions that suited our ancestors have not necessarily aged well, as they say, and are ill-fitted for modern circumstances and sensibilities. The theologian Randall C. Bailey agrees that in the Bible,

> "The Word of God,"…gives it a sense of universalism and timelessness and elevates it as a reality above a culture…Too often we have failed to look at the Biblical text as a cultural production within its own time and geographical location, and we have not recognized that our interpretations of the biblical text have been prodded and shaped by our cultural understandings and time.[86]

Cultural differences from the Bible can include prostitution and incest. Today, many consider both morally unacceptable. For example, in the Old Testament, Naomi, the mother-in-law

---

86 Randall C. Bailey, "The Bible as a text of Cultures," *The People's Bible,* edited by Curtiss Paul DeYoung et al., 13–22. Minneapolis: Fortress Press, 2009.

of Ruth, suggested the idea of Ruth's prostitution with Boaz, a landlord. They were suffering from famine, and they needed to survive. Naomi tells Ruth, "Now wash and anoint yourself, and put on your best clothes go down to the threshing floor; but do not make yourself known to the man until he has finished eating and drinking. When he lies down, observe the place where he lies; then, go and uncover his feet and lie down; and he will tell you what to do" (Ruth 3:3–4).

Historical and cultural differences should also apply to the Quran. Because Muslims believe that the Quran is purely God's words, it becomes harder to read it through those two lenses. Yet, it's not impossible.

One might argue that the culture of the Quran is almost the same as the Arab culture today, but it is not. An example of a cultural difference is hijab, the female headscarf. In a TED talk, Samina Ali says,

> The early Muslim scholars ruled that a woman's way of dress should be based on two considerations:
>
> 1. A woman's function in society. Her role, what we might consider her job.
>
> 2. And the society's specific customs.
>
> Muslims like to take historical rulings and apply them to the modern.[87]

---

87 *TED*, "What does the Quran say about a Muslim woman's hijab?" Feb 10, 2017, video, 17:47.

She then elaborates, wearing a veil in the age of Al-Jahiliyyah of the fifth century was highly recommended to protect non-free, slave women from being molested. She adds, back then, bathrooms were outside the house, and some men saw this as their opportunity to sexually harass women. However, they would not mess with a woman wearing a Jilbab, a type of clothing that manifested social status. Of course, slave women could not wear the same attire to prevent this from happening. Consequently, when this matter was brought up to the Prophet, a veil was the solution.[88] One might argue that the culture then and now is the same Arab culture. However, infanticide was widely culturally accepted then, but it is not now.

When the father of my friend, Amjaad, died, she sobbed to me, saying, "I didn't talk to him, Tamar. He refused to see me ever since I removed my hijab two years ago." She is still living with that guilt because her parents choose to interpret the Quran the way most people do. Some also comment on her social media stories with horrible things like, "You are honoring your father in his grave with the way you dress up now," followed by offensive slurs. They interpret religion in a way that suits their own beliefs and needs.

We change. The world changes. Thus, when reading the Holy Books, we should be aware of the traditions and customs that were historically and culturally accepted in the times these books were written. This way, extremely religious people can perhaps tolerate others of different beliefs as long as they respect each other's personal space.

---

88 Ibid.

THE ONE TRUE RELIGION

More than half of the global population reports affiliation with Christianity or Islam. Four times as many people align with folk religions as those who identify as Jewish. Only 0.2 percent identify themselves as Jewish.[89] But, does it matter? Why do we divide rather than unite?

Believers of the three monotheistic religions—Judaism, Christianity, and Islam—often hold their religion as the one true religion, and this is where the problem lies. Jews argue that they are God's chosen people, according to the Torah. As for Christianity, Christians believe that Jesus reincarnated to save his children. There are many instances in the New Testamant where the Pharisees —"member(s) of a Jewish religious party that flourished in Palestine during the latter part of the Second Temple period (515 BCE–70 CE)"[90]—argued with Jesus or asked him about the Laws of Moses. In some cases, Jesus made some amendments to these laws. Similarly, the idea that Islam came after Christianity makes it seem like Christianity is a fraud. As if Islam came to fix some aspects of Christianity. Thus, Islam should be the true one religion, right?

Is one religion the truest? Are they all equal? Are none of them true? It does not matter what one believes, for they chose what makes them the happiest. Unfortunately, it is not that simple, and I wish it were. Why do people use religion to separate instead of connecting with one another? The division contradicts the idea of religion. Loving each other;

---

89 "Religious Composition by Country, 2010–2050," Pew Research Center's Religion & Public Life Project, accessed September 21, 2020.

90 *Encyclopedia Britannica*, s.v. "Pharisee," accessed September 21, 2020.

living peacefully with each other; being good to each other. Why do we find it hard to tolerate each other when religion requests it of us?

THE BATTLE OF RELIGIONS CONTINUES

It's ironic when prejudice towards people of different religions is too deep. Then, people fight against each other in a meaningless battle of increasing the numbers of that religious group.

In a Netflix drama based on the memoir of Deborah Feldman, *Unorthodox*, the main character, Esther Haas, is forced to marry someone she doesn't like at a young age. She justifies it saying, "[Orthodox women] are rebuilding the six million lost [Jews]" in the Holocaust.[91] As for Christians, I always hear Christians in Palestine saying,

"Oh, I'm so glad they are having a baby! The Christian percentage in this country must increase."

Even some Muslims believe they should increase the number of Muslims. According to a Hadith—a collection of the words, actions, and the silent approval of the Prophet Muhammad—the prophet says in a Hadith: "Marry and have children because I will vie the nations in number by you on the Day of Resurrection."[92] After all, children are a blessing. For example, "Wealth and children are the ornaments of this present life.

---

91   *Unorthodox*, directed by Maria Schrader, written by Anna Winger, Alexa Karolinska, and Daniel Hendler, inspired by Deborah Feldman's 2012 autobiography, debuted on March 26, 2020, on Netflix.

92   "الودود الولود في ميزان العدل الرباني،" جريدة الدستور الاردنية, accessed September 23, 2020.

But the things that last and good deeds, are better with your Lord in reward and hope" (Al-Kahf 18:46).

They all want to increase their numbers even when they cannot afford it economically and intellectually in some cases. To add, they consider abortion a sin, and one still hears about immature babies thrown in dumpsters.

These people of God believe in religious exclusivism, yet they tend to forget that all the monotheistic religions mentioned here are similar in their ideas. Although the similarities between these three religions are more than their differences, people focus on the differences more. Sometimes, it can even be in the same religion itself. The truest blood in Judaism, Sunnah and Shi'a in Islam, and the many denominations in Christianity are the best examples for insisting on division. I sincerely wish to live and witness a Christmas in Bethlehem city when Palestinian Christians do not fight each other in the Nativity Church, where Jesus was born, on whose spot this is for.

The conclusion is again the same, we divide rather than unite, and as cheesy as it may sound, "In unity there is strength."

THE STRUCTURE OF POWER

I grew up Christian, but it's tough when you're not spiritual.

Believing in God isn't and has never been easy for me. However, when I ask myself, *Who is God?*, the best answer I could think of is, *God is love and goodness.* That's what makes sense, at least to me. Some details don't and shouldn't matter because, again, historical and cultural differences exist. The problem is with those who interpret religion in connotations to power. Power is the source of destruction to many things. Power in religion is one of them, and there shouldn't be a polarization of power in religion for historical and social reasons.

Historically, many people used their religious power to conquer other nations. One example is the Crusades, "a series of campaigns between 1095 and 1270 to retake Jerusalem from the Turks."[93] These Europeans considered the war in the name of the Holy God. "The First Crusade resulted in the formation of the crusader states in the Levant (the eastern Mediterranean), which were initially governed, and in small part populated, by settlers from Europe."[94] They conquered lands and enforced new laws.

Moreover, the Early Islamic Conquests (622–750 AD) has the name "Islamic" in the title. Here, religion becomes an excuse to enforce power, conquer the land, and in some cases, oppress people. In these conquests,

- "Islam spread through military conquest, trade, pilgrimage, and missionaries.

- Arab Muslim forces conquered vast territories and built imperial structures over time."[95]

---

93 James Peter. Burkholder, Donald Jay Grout, and Claude Victor. Palisca, *A History of Western Music,* 65.

94 Susanna Throop, "The Impact of the Crusades," Smarthistory, accessed September 22, 2020.

95 "The Rise of Islamic Empires and States (Article)," Khan Academy (Khan Academy), accessed September 22, 2020.

In this case, religious military power helped the spread of Islam.

Both the crusades and conquests are not nearly as horrific as the modern version. For example, the Islamic State in Iraq and Levant (ISIL) murdered innocent people in cold blood, raped women violently without mercy, kidnapped clueless children ruthlessly, and committed other horrific crimes in the name of religion even when they do not represent Islam. Their interpretation of it is sickening. To further explain,

> ISIL focuses on the idea of "jihad," defined by them as "Holy war." However, in the Qur'an, *jihad* (meaning simply "struggle" or "striving" in Arabic) is not used to justify killing innocents or to condone violent behavior; even when used specifically concerning war. *Jihad*, according to the Qur'an, is permissible only as defensive action when the Muslim community is directly attacked. Additionally, prophetic sayings and injunctions by the first Islamic caliphs forbid targeting civilians, specifically women and children.[96]

Thus, I've realized that the problem lies in the people who hold power and interpret their Holy books according to what suits their position.

Other than what history tells us about power structures and its religious abuse, today, we still use that structure socially to discriminate against other religions. The expectation of a

---

96 "An Overview of ISIS," Islamic Networks Group (ING), accessed September 22, 2020, https://ing.org/an-overview-of-isis/.

wife is to carry her husband's name in the Middle East and Palestine. If he was Muslim, she has to convert to Islam in case she wasn't.

A few years back, I was sitting with members of my extended family who were looking at wedding videos of a bride they know. She's Christian. The groom is Muslim. Usually, when my family sees pictures and videos of weddings, they would comment on the beauty of the bride and setting. However, that time was different. They were commenting on one thing: the bride and the groom's different religions. One of my family members said,

"How does she have the audacity to marry a Muslim man? Even worse! How are both their families happy, cheering, and dancing throughout the wedding?

"This is so wrong. They are making it seem like it's okay for something like this to happen," said a very educated member surprisingly.

Even in a marriage that's supposed to be about equality and reciprocity, there still exists some structural power. Such people want that difference. If they didn't want it, the idea of two people of different religions in love shouldn't bother them.

From that moment on, the world depicted its true gloomy colors to me. Peace signs and rainbows are merely some shades of grey clumped together, for reality is, we're trapped in a sublime, dark, dull room deprived of any traces of sunlight. Only when one penetrates its walls they can witness the bright green, shiny, leafy vines curling around it and dangling above it—a beautiful, peaceful haven. If one crushes hatred and power structure with their bare feet with love, the golden rays of the sun eventually smoothly paint their pale faces with warmth. They would reunite with the picturesque nature and confront the uncanniness of life.

LOVE IS UNIVERSAL.

"I left my family for the man I love," the young Palestinian woman tells me.

Today, Dima (not her real name) has a family of her own. Not so long ago, the life she shares with two beautiful young daughters and their father—Dima's husband—seemed impossible. And if the forces working against them had succeeded, it truly would have been.

Dima, you see, is a Christian. The man she loves and married is Muslim. And while I believe that no interpretation of religion should draw forbidden lines between two people in love, I understand that my view is not popular in my culture.

Her lover was put in a cold, dim jail cell after her family accused him of kidnapping Dima.

"I was given a choice to go home with my parents or go to the safe house," says Dima. The safe house is a shelter for women suffering from domestic violence. "I chose the safe house to get things done with my husband…It wasn't just my parents, it was an entire society," she continues.

At the safe house, where most of the women were priorly domestically abused, she finds herself in deep sorrow. She feels lonely and stressed. However, this soon changes when her lover calls her from prison. She says that in one phone call, "He gave [her] hope." He told her he is working hard to get her out of the safe house and that she shouldn't give up. So, she "stayed strong for him."

"I was released two months after my parents agreed on giving us a chance to be together," she reminisces.

At that moment, it seemed like a dream come true, and Dima finally began to see some bright light at the end of a long, endless tunnel. That one dim candlelight dispersed the dark shadows roaming around her.

"After I got out [of the safe house], my parents changed their mind and wanted to send me to America to live with my uncle," she recalls. "I then ran away again with [my lover]. We hid in different places for fifteen days before we were caught by the Palestinian Preventive Security. Afterward, I again chose the safe house and stayed there for another two months." Then, she adds, "We managed to get married while I was at the safe house…We were clever, and we were able to get our marriage contract confirmation from the court, and of course, secretly done."

It was disappointing to Dima that she and the love of her life "were rejected by everyone."

Dima's father-in-law died, and the people loved to conspire and make it seem like she had something to do with it. However, it wasn't like that. She explains that her father-in-law "had a disease in his heart, but he was fine. The Palestinian

Preventive Security took him as a way to make us turn ourselves in to the authorities. On the same day, he got tired and stayed in the hospital for ten days and then passed away."

Many blamed her for the death of her father-in-law. The story shared amongst people was, "Dima killed her father." They would say, "He had a stroke after she escaped from the safe house." In reality, it wasn't even her father who died. Until today, her family refuses to see her, and people keep saying horrible things about her. They even determined that she has a bad reputation and marked her with a red dot on her forehead. It is ironic because Dima says, "The person they keep talking about doesn't resemble who I really am."

I believe Dima and her husband succeeded. They did not give up, and they didn't end up dead like those who fought back. After marriage, Dima graduated and had children. She has the most adorable two little daughters. I vividly recall her taking the stairs at BU with one hand on her belly protecting her first unborn daughter.

Dima and her husband are happy about their decision because they chose to stay with the love of their life regardless of everyone who told them not to. She only wishes she could see her parents and sisters. Her parents refuse to see her even though she misses them. That's an example of love beating all odds, including prejudicial religious beliefs.

* * *

Religion may not convince those who purely think logically and scientifically. But, when people read through the historical and cultural lens, religion would make more sense. Regardless, one should choose whatever suits their needs best. The facts given above urge us to think critically about everything rather than believe in the given information. Some people comfortably believe in a divine power that has created them. Others don't need spirituality. My friend Mustapha says, "Sometimes, we tend to believe in the things that we know are absurd just because they make us happy." The problem lies in those who read religion in a way that marginalizes women and people of a different race, color, and sexual orientation.

Men's interpretation of religion can oppress women. In the Quran, for instance, "الرِّجَالُ قَوَّامُونَ عَلَى النِّسَاءِ" or "Men are the protectors and maintainers of women" (An Nissa 4:34). In Arabic the verse can sound like: men are more powerful and capable than women. Some chose this translation to obtain a sense of power. In reality, it says that men should support women, and let us not forget that part of this is cultural and historical. Back then, and in many cases, it was unsafe for the women to work outside the house to support a family. A woman could easily get molested without social status. Same for marrying four wives. It protected women. It's ironic. Women still get sexually harassed every day in Palestine, especially verbally. I also hear at least one story a month of a woman raped in Palestine or other neighboring countries.

Both the Quran and the Bible refer to slavery and the merciful and humane rules of having a slave. However, back then, it was culturally the norm to have a slave, but that does not justify racism or slavery anywhere and anytime. Similarly, homosexuality was not culturally or historically accepted. It is still not today in many places, yet it is more accepted than it used to be in some countries.

Thus, we should stop referring to those historic periods nationalistically, ignoring the historical and cultural differences, and aiming to apply them in our everyday lives in the twenty-first century.

TAKEAWAYS

- Nationalism can be toxic if connected to extreme religious beliefs.

- Reading Holy Books through the historical and cultural lens is vital.

- No religion is the truest.

- Religions have one main message: be good and love others.

- Religion is not interested in power structures.

- Religion should unite rather than divide.

- Love is above toxic religious beliefs.

CHAPTER FIVE

THE FEMALE NARRATIVE

—

"You have to be a superwoman at home," Sama's husband tells her.

Sama (not her real name), a young Palestinian woman in her twenties, is put in a cage. She moved from her father's cage to her husband's. She's like a small bird with cut wings. The owners think it's safer and better for her to stay in their golden cages. "It's for your own good," they tell her.

But I want to fly and see the world, she thinks to herself. Instead, she says, "You're right! I love you both, and you know what's best for me."

Her husband says, "I love you too," but hurts her in bed. "Men's pleasure matters the most," he says. He disagrees with her when she says, "But I'm a feminist! And it's not my job to only give pleasure. You're supposed to please me too—reciprocity." He hates when she calls herself a "feminist." He refuses to let her work an hour away from home despite "very good job offers." He doesn't communicate with her, and when he does, he only talks about her "flaws." He complains about her making dinner late to his mom without mentioning it to her. She says he simply expects her to be a "superwoman at home." That's a glimpse of some Palestinian women's lives.

French feminist theorist Simone de Beauvoir studied the existential forces used to subjugate women to men throughout history. First published in 1949, her book, *The Second Sex,* challenges the societal, religious, and political patriarchies designed to justify women's inferior status throughout history. Gender roles are based on the power structure, de Beauvoir observed. By restricting women to the domestic sphere while men work in the public sphere, men attain, and retain financial power. Men become transcendent, while women remain immanent.[97]

In countries around the world, women have demanded and received the freedom to work outside the domestic sphere. In some societies, it truly is possible—even commonplace—for women to achieve financial independence if they choose. Financial equality, however, continues to elude us. "Data from 2015 points to a significant gender pay gap, with women's median daily wage (USD $21.2) comprising seventy-six percent of the median daily wage for men (USD $27.8)."[98] It seems that even when we think we're uncaged and free to chart our flight paths, we discover a net overhead to prevent us from rising as high as our male counterparts. A working Palestinian woman may have money, but a Palestinian man has more of it and, therefore, the power is his. And not just

---

97 Simone De Beauvoir, "The Second Sex," *Vintage Classic* 3. no. 1 (2011).

98 International Labour Organization, "Exploring the gender pay gap in Occupied Palestinian Territory: A qualitative study of the education sector," *Policy Brief 2016,* 2.

in the boardroom. In the bedroom, her engendered role is to give pleasure. His role is to receive it.

The fact is, the Palestinian society has been discriminating against women, Otherizing them, and expecting them to fit into certain gender roles. Those expectations lasted for so long that we have normalized them. Can a new generation of feminists change that?

TO BE A WOMAN IN PALESTINE

It's uncanny for a woman to consider herself a feminist in a patriarchal world. Many misinterpret feminism. It's never about women having more rights than men. It's not about hating men. It's about being equal to men because women aren't. Witnessing and experiencing the oppression, sexism, and misogyny towards women is difficult. Thus, like all the women who say they need to be equal to men, I stand on their side.

THE OTHER

Living in a world where women are equal to men may seem utopian. Yet, oppression should not come from the label of the Other, the object rather than the subject. What is it like to be the Other in Palestine, and how are men's gazes related to that?

In my search for an answer to this question, I've asked a dear feminist friend to tell me what it is like to be a woman in Palestine. By her request, her identity has been protected to enable her to speak freely. "As a woman born and raised in

Palestine, I had many challenges in fighting the patriarchal society," she says. "Growing up, I have always been told not to go places alone, not to walk by myself, not to wear normal clothes which some people call revealing." She adds she had to be careful about how to sit. Even the simple act of sitting down was anything but simple during my friend's teenage years.

"Never open your legs. Always keep them close to each other whether you're wearing jeans or a skirt," her parents told her.

"Whatever you do, make sure you have a good reputation," her mother emphasized repeatedly.

"I never loved my teens like other people." She paused and continued, "I never dated. I never hung out with guys if my brothers weren't with me. One time, my brother was about to slap me just because I was talking to a guy. My parents stood there without any action thinking, 'Your brother knows how guys think. He is protecting you.'"

"He is protecting you," she repeated. The words remain as painful today as they ever were.

"I was raised with the idea that I would never be capable of protecting myself. No matter how strong I showed them I was, I was always treated like a girl who would not know what to do in difficult situations," she said, adding,

> Many girls go through more difficult circumstances. I had a classmate in the seventh grade who was not allowed to shave her arms because guys would find that sexy! Another whom her brother hit and was allowed

to because she fell in love with a sweet boy. A girl who was not allowed to go out with her fiancé to have a cup of coffee because they are not yet married. A girl who, at the age of eighteen, had to decide whether to get married or stay at home and be hit by her father every day just because she was born a girl and not a boy.

And the stories go on and on.

The gaze of toxic masculinity others Palestinian women. It criticizes women who step outside the norm—outside who they are "supposed to be." The gaze can come from other women too. And when it does, it's even worse.

I've always been afraid of slipping and doing something the Other is expected to do. An example would be hugging my friends who identify as males. Anything can turn me into a "bad woman," and I've always feared that. When talking about gender roles, Simone de Beauvoir says women are given a certain role, and the expectation is that they fit into that role. If they play an "evil" role, they will be regarded as "bad women."[99] Mistakenly, I thought I was right when I tried to distance myself from males fearing falling into that trap, and it's an error of a whole society—Othering women.

TRANSCENDENCE VS. IMMINENCE

Gender roles in patriarchy: Men are active. They do. They create. Women are inactive. They don't do. They maintain. They are

---

99 Simone De Beauvoir, *The Second Sex*, trans. H. M. Parshley. (New York: Alfred A. Knopf, 1953), 1407.

passive. This is a summary of Simone de Beauvoir's differentiation between transcendence and imminence. Beauvoir says, "All human existence is transcendence and immanence at the same time; to go beyond itself, it must maintain itself; to thrust itself toward the future, it must integrate the past into itself."[100]

Sama is an example of a woman who wants to be transcendent, but the society suppresses her desires. Despite her small, slim body, she has the potential to do a lot. Instead of looking down at the street with the wind blowing her straight, short, shiny, dark hair, she can look up and walk confidently because of the woman she is.

Sama is a Palestinian friend and classmate. She grew up in a strict, conservative environment. At the age of sixteen, she spent about a year in an American high school as part of the Youth Exchange and Study (YES) program by the Amideast. She had a hard time convincing her father that this is a good opportunity for her, and it was. She says, "I studied so hard for the English grammar exam we had to do and applied." They interviewed her multiple times before she finally got accepted.

She says, "When I first heard about the YES program, I thought I could discuss applying to it with my father, and it wasn't easy." She thought he would immediately say no. However, "he underestimated [her] abilities." Therefore, the father ended up signing his approval. He believed that she will not be able to make it, especially as a United Nations Relief and Works Agency (UNRWA) student at a school for Palestinian refugees. "UNRWA schools aren't the best when it comes to English," she says.

---

100 Simone De Beauvoir, *The Second Sex*, Trans. Constance Borde and Sheila Malovany Chevallier. (New York: Vintage, 2011).

Sama ended up getting married about two years after traveling to the US. She was a first-year student at college. She married traditionally, meaning her current husband asked for her hand. She says, "We didn't get to date much." It was official from the start. Still, she says, "It was my choice, and no one forced me to accept him at all. I did accept getting engaged after one month of meeting him."

Sama's strict father has always demanded much of her. Both her parents are refugees. Her father has had some terrible experiences. Before turning twenty-five years old, her father lost two brothers who are considered Palestinian martyrs and his father, who was even stricter. One of the brothers died due to an injured leg. He got shot by an Israeli soldier going on a protest against a decision made by Ariel Sharon, the eleventh Prime Mister of Israel.

Sama's other uncle was a Business Administration senior at Bethlehem University and the founder of its environmental club. "He got shot right between his eyes by an Israeli soldier at a protest," says Sama. The starting point of that protest was from Bethlehem University. It was against the Israeli digging of a tunnel under the Aqsa Mosque—an important religious monument for Muslims all over the world. Today, he has a special memorial at the very entrance of the university.

Sama was not conscious of this then. She was only three years old. However, as she grew up, she became aware of how these incidents have affected her father. She witnessed the "bad life" her mother had to endure with her dad and his traumas. Thus, to escape her dad's trauma, Sama developed a dream. She became obsessed with the idea of going to the US.

When she was about to leave, she had some contrastive feelings. She was delighted to leave her strict dad and achieve her dream. At the same time, she was sad she had to leave her mother and sisters. Yet, this was a "new beginning" for her.

In the US, Sama bloomed like a flower that desperately needed water. She dug deep into herself and figured that she is somebody. In the US, others appreciated her for the person she is—something people barely do in the Palestinian society. She tells me, "I was successful there, and it was the most productive year *ever* in my life. I felt like I am somebody—a productive person. I had a lot of achievements. I did one hundred hours of volunteering there. I won a gold medal from the YES program. I won a plot essay, and I received a certificate from the US department." She emphasized, "The freedom out there made me feel like a butterfly. It wasn't the freedom of dressing up the way you want or going out wherever you want. You just have more chances to do a lot of things. I don't know why, but you have a lot of chances. You are encouraged out there. It's not like here. People don't encourage here."

Sama won. She got what she wanted, but she had to go back to reality. The road got bumpy, and her dreams shattered. She told me, "One's energy is different in the US." After she slowly turned into a beautiful rose, she suddenly withered and died. "There, people give you steps to move forward and start things. Here, everything is criticized," she adds. Therefore, she chose a normal life. She got married, graduated, and figured it was time to have babies. But she found out she has an ovary problem, and it is unlikely for her to have children. Her in-laws still push her to this day to do the impossible and have a baby. She was shocked when her in-laws gave her certain "recipes that supposedly help a woman have a child." A normal life for a Palestinian woman.

This is an example of antagonism within Palestine—discrimination against women in everyday life. To explain this in feminist ideology, Sama feels passive in Palestine. Her family was encouraged by the idea of her marrying at a young age. Even though Sama sees this as an escape from her father's control, she leads a typical social way of life. According to de Beauvoir, "Since man occupies a privileged situation in this world, he is in a position to show his love actively; very often he supports the woman or at least helps her; in marrying her, he gives her social standing; he makes her presents; his independent economic and social positions allow him to take the initiative and think up contrivances."[101] Sama told me that her husband doesn't like the idea of her supporting the house. He believes that society expects him to do that part, for he rejects to be imminent rather than transcendent. If Sama makes more money than him, the power and privilege would reverse, and the husband wouldn't have that power that is derived economically.

Relationships are about love and reciprocity. There shouldn't be any power structure in relationships. The couple should be transcendent.

SEXUAL HARASSMENT AND THE SEPARATION OF GENDERS

"Fifty percent of Palestinian women and sixty-three percent of Palestinian men agreed that a woman should tolerate violence to keep the family together."[102] Sexual harassment in Palestine is tolerated and accepted, but it should not be.

---

101 De Beauvoir, *The Second Sex*, trans. H. M. Parshley, 1411.

102 UN Women Palestine, "Facts and Figures: Ending Violence against Women," accessed October 3, 2020.

Verbal sexual harassment and catcalling are familiar to many Palestinian women. It can happen anywhere in the world, no matter how developed a country is. Any type of sexual harassment (physical, verbal, cyber, etc.) can be severe on a women's psyche. Sexual harassment, in its many forms, is nonconsensual. Thus, sexual harassment can happen in relationships if one side does not consent to the sexual act.

Why do we, women, have to experience that? Why do some of us feel like they have to hide from the world and cover their souls and bodies with the sand of the beach that almost suffocates them? Why is the relationship between woman and man not reciprocal?

In Palestine, it is popular to have all-boy and all-girl schools. Coeducational schools represent 29 percent of total schools in Palestine, all-boys' schools are 37 percent, and all-girls' schools are 53 percent.[103] Thus, there is a huge percentage of students who don't interact with the opposite sex before seeking higher education. Some of these males might view women as merely object later on in life, which Otherizes women.

I always see videos on social media of men commenting on a woman fully covered, peacefully walking down the street, trying to avoid their gaze. In these videos, the men say, "I am human! I have no control over my emotions and desires." Such men are so sexually suppressed that they harass and rape innocent women. Eventually, the women are the ones to blame for what they were wearing or saying. As for some of the females

103 WikiMiki, "Education in the State of Palestine." Accessed October 3, 2020.

that grow up in all-girl schools, their ultimate goal would be finding the "perfect husband," marrying, and becoming mothers. Going to an all-girls' school for my tertiary education, most of the gossip I've heard was annoyingly about boys.

During a Bethlehem festival, a professor at Bethlehem University (BU) calls for a separation between men and women at the festival in a Facebook post. He argued that it would prevent sexual harassment. His wife was one of the victims. However, asking for this type of segregation is extremely problematic as it normalizes sexual harassment. Unfortunately, the Palestinian government has been doing it for years. For example, at public concerts—like those of Mohammed Assaf—precautionary procedures were taken to separate men and women. Women were sexually violated at one of these concerts earlier. It becomes comfortable to have barriers. Women feel safer, and men do whatever they want outside that separation.

Another form of problematic segregation between genders is Pink Cafe. Pink Cafe is a cafe that opened for a while in Beit Sahour designed specifically for women. It mimics the masculine Arab cafes. People agree that only men are allowed to visit such cafe's where they smoke Hookah, play cards, board games, and drink tea or coffee. It is a man's zone. No woman dares to think of going there until one day, a male entrepreneur decides to dedicate such a cafe for women only. When my friends and I heard about it as freshmen at BU, we got excited. We were thinking, finally, a turning point. We go there, and the place is submerged in pink, which my close friend Jowana dislikes. She had to hate the color pink because society agreed, "pink is for girls."

The color of the cafe is not the main point here. What bothers me is how I thought of this cafe as a step forward. At least that is what most of the women thought of it. However, that cafe was just another step towards the normalization of the separation of the two genders. Even to those who thought this cafe was good for Palestinian women it did not last long. Why? The name cafe is still associated with a place for men only. When I went there, I was too scared to tell my parents I was going to the cafe. I was too afraid to have that bad reputation.

Tell me why all the persecuted Palestinian women I have interviewed for this book refused to keep their real names. Why did they feel it unsafe to reveal their identities? It is because of how dangerous our society could be. It comes with its consequences not only in Palestine but anywhere else. It's because of this patriarchal society that has to have control over women, what they say, and what they do.

To wrap this up, Palestinians believe that to avoid sexual harassment, there has to be a separation between men and women. However, this is not the solution to the problem. On the contrary, this normalizes the problem.

HOPE

Humans try to find hope in life despite all the problems they face. Big institutions with power must work to give hope to the people.

Women need that hope, and their hope is within the Lutheran Church and its judicial system. The Evangelical Lutheran

Church in Jordan and the Holy Land (ELCJHL) helps women of different religions, denominations, or other religious beliefs. Humanity comes first.

The Evangelical Lutheran Church is one of the main reasons why I wrote this book. The Evangelical Lutheran Church in America (ELCA) is covering my International Women Leaders scholarship at California Lutheran University. If it weren't for them, it would be harder to have a positive impact on my society. Fortunately, the ELCJHL holds many events and conferences for Palestinian women too.

On September 21, 2019, the Woman's Desk of the ELCJHL held a workshop titled, *The status of Palestinian Woman's Rights and the Implementing implementation of the Convention on the Elimination of All Forms of Discrimination Against Woman* (CEDAW). I randomly met Judge Scarlet Bishara, the first female judge in the Ecclesiastical Court of the Evangelical Lutheran Church, at the United Nations (UN) headquarters in New York City. "It's so good to see someone from home!" I recall telling her. Judge Bishara was a panel presenter at the UN's 63rd Commission on the Status of Women. From the panel, I learned CEDAW is empowering Palestinian women and helping them fight for their rights. I was proud of my Church and its representatives at the UN.

Another activity the Woman's Desk does is the Thursdays in Black campaign: towards a world without rape and violence. In this peaceful protest, women wore black on Thursdays to challenge attitudes that cause violence and raise awareness about it. In the Palestinian culture, like many others, people wear black to mourn. Here, the woman wore black to mourn women affected, harmed, or killed by sexual violence. It is a form of protest. ELCJHL also holds conferences like Gender Justice from a Religious Perspective. This conference was held on June 13, 2019 to discuss gender injustice from a Christian and Muslim point of view. Thus, the ELCJHL is one platform that speaks for the rights of Palestinian women.

In her research, *Religious Actors Promoting Gender Equality Through Personal Status Laws in Palestine: The ELCJHL Model*, Judge Bishara proposes utilizing "the Lutheran Gender Justice Family Law as a model."[104] She says, "This new church constitution is unique in the Middle Eastern context, dealing with family matters such as marriage, marital finances, custody, alimony, separation, divorce, and inheritance from the perspective of gender justice and equality."[105] This model was then used in other legal Christian systems because of its efficiency.

TAKEAWAYS

- Women are Otherized by the masculine gaze.

- Women shouldn't be perceived as imminent, but rather transcendent.

- Sexual harassment leads to segregation between genders and shouldn't be normalized.

- The Evangelical Lutheran Church gives hope to women.

---

104 Mitri Raheb, *Middle Eastern Women: The Intersection of Law, Culture and Religion* (Bethlehem: Diyar Publisher, 2020).

105 Ibid.

CHAPTER SIX

ASPECTS OF PALESTINIAN RACISM

———

"Dad, why do these people have this dark color?" a Palestinian child asks.

"Their parents forgot them in the oven, Baba," answers the father.[106]

"I bought a big box of Ras El Abed today," my uncle would say. As children, my siblings and I would come running. To us, Ras El Abed meant only one thing: candy. This popular Middle Eastern treat starts with a sweet, soft cookie on the bottom, then topped with whipped cream and enrobed in creamy milk chocolate. Its shape resembles a bald head. In our sweet innocence, we did not know Ras El Abed translates to *a slave's head*.

As a Palestinian, you, too, might be saying racist slurs without even knowing it. What is racism? Does racism exist in

———

106 Maryam Abu Khaled (@maryamabukhaled1), "العنصرية الغير مقصودة والغير مباشرة بعد معنا وقت," Instagram photo, June 5, 2020.

Palestine? Why do we need to abolish it? Is it possible to hold racist views against our own race?

* * *

RACISM IN THE ARAB WORLD AND PALESTINE

The Anti-Defamation League (ADL) defines racism as "the belief that a particular race is superior or inferior to another, that a person's social and moral traits are predetermined by his or her inborn biological characteristics. Racial separatism is the belief, most of the time, based on racism, that different races should remain segregated and apart from one another."[107]

Maryam Abu Khaled is an influencer and Instagram advocate for Black voices. She has dealt with racism her entire life. She has big, curly hair and beautiful round, black eyes. As an Afro-Palestinian child, she was often bullied for her black skin. Maryam shares some of her experiences on her Instagram to raise awareness about racism in Palestine. In one of her videos, she comments that others have perceived her as ugly because of her skin color.[108] As a child, her friend's mother warned her daughter, saying, "Come back home and stop playing under the sun. You don't want to burn and become like Maryam."[109]

Maryam adds that others debated whether "bleaching black in chlorine water" would turn them white or not.[110] Maryam

---

107 "Racism," Anti-Defamation League, accessed September 28, 2020.

108 Abu Khaled, "العنصرية الغير مقصودة."

109 Ibid.

110 Ibid.

says this sentiment is strong and needs to stop. The Arab world perceives white as beautiful because—with predominantly fair, blonde, blue-eyed models—the Western world influences international beauty standards. If the media portrays white beautiful and pure, then we can perceive Black as ugly or dirty by default.

TOWARDS BLACK PEOPLE

My mom, not appreciating the fact that I hang out with African American or African friends in the US, comments on their skin color and chooses to stereotype.

"Beware of the slaves," my maternal grandma also warned me from African Americans before traveling to the US for the first time.

Joking about skin color is racist. The many forms of racism are unacceptable and should stop before they become normalized in the Palestinian/Arab region.

The Black community in Palestine experiences racism on a daily basis. To create their own sense of racial superiority and power, many Arabs discriminate against the Afro community and direct ethnic epithets towards them, including offensive slurs, the N-word, and Blackface.

The Afro-Palestinian community is small. It consists of 350–450 people, mostly centered in Jerusalem.[111] [112] "The

---

111   Ilan Ben Zion, "The Old City's African Secret," *The Times of Israel,* April 6, 2014.

112   Joharah Baker, "The African-Palestinians: Muslim Pilgrims Who Never Went Home," *The New Arab,* December 26, 2014

Arab slave trade in Africans (not to mention Persians, Jews, Caucasians, Abyssinians, and others) became so extensive that by the middle of the ninth century, there were as many as three million Africans enslaved in the Middle East."[113] Despite the small number, Palestinians discriminate against the Black Palestinian society.

Ali Jiddah, a Black Palestinian, says, "To identify ourselves, we say we are Afro-Palestinians. We were born here [in Palestine]. We grew up here. We have the same history as Palestinians."[114] Jiddah acknowledges the oppression of Palestinians. He argues that both the occupation and the color double oppress Afro-Palestinians.[115]

It is easy to assume that because the African community is tiny in Palestine, we aren't racist. I despise labeling people and being labeled, but ironically, Arabs are considered people of color too in the US, for example. That was one of the first moments I started questioning why Palestinians and Arabs are racist in general, and this was just the beginning.

In May 2020, a heatwave hit Palestine, and it was too hot for anyone to handle. As a result, I recall one of my friends posting a picture on Facebook (FB) of a completely, extremely black baby troll with full black eyes and a few black, kinky strands of hair. Underneath the picture, the caption said, "A Palestinian child born this afternoon."

---

113 Charmaine Seitz, "Pilgrimage to a New Self: The African Quarter and its people," *Institute for Palestine Studies*, no. 16 (2020): 43.

114 *AP Archive*, "Jerusalem's Afro Palestinians feel more integrated," Feb 5, 2017, video, 4:25.

115 Ibid.

When I confronted her and told her this is not appropriate, her response was, "The baby is only a joke because of the high temperature. Nothing else. Believe me." She wasn't the only person on FB who posted the same meme in the same week. A couple of days later, the same friend posts another picture of a dark grey cat with her kittens arranged from the lightest to the darkest with the caption, "The mom is out of ink." We've seen similar memes but with human babies, and it never stops.

THE N-WORD

Racial epithets commonly directed toward members of the Black community in Palestine are weapons for pain and humiliation. Some who use ethnic slurs are ignorant of the words' racist roots, though the damage is no less severe.

One of my Arab acquaintances posted a video of his three-year-old niece on social media. In the video, the little girl smiles adoringly at her beloved uncle as he teaches her to say the N-word.

"Say, f*ck you [N-word]," he yells aggressively.

She repeats loudly and proudly. He giggles.

"Say it again," he tells her. Again, she does exactly as instructed.

It was disturbing to watch. The clueless child was trying to make her twenty-six-year-old uncle happy. She loved pleasing him and hearing his laugh. She had no idea her dear uncle was exploiting her innocence and abusing not only her trust but also, perhaps, the trust of her parent, who left her in his care. She is not his child. The choice to expose her to this vile word, much less teach it to her, was not his choice to make. Yet he did. He chose the words, coerced them from her innocent lips, and shared them with the world.

I, for one, had a few words of my own to express. I could not sit by and watch without speaking up on behalf of the little girl. I angrily pounded my thoughts into my keyboard and watched them display on my phone screen. Knowing how violent and aggressive he is, I did not expect a positive, understanding response. He answered, "Dude, chill. Just coz you live in the US and the 'N-word' there is bad doesn't mean I can't say it as a joke. Be liberal. Relax."

And that was it. I unfriended him—on social media and in life.

This man completely dismissed the horrific history behind the word. I hope the rest of the world never forgets it. After the Atlantic Slave trade, ten to twelve million Black people were transported from their own African homes to be slaves in the western world from the sixteenth until the nineteenth century.[116] Even when this transportation and the horrible acts done towards slaves ended, it did not get easy still. Black people in America, for example, are humiliated on a daily basis, and a simple example is the constant use of the N-word by white people towards African Americans. According to the Article "Who has the 'Right' to Use the N-Word?":

---

116 Thomas Lewis, s.v. "Transatlantic Slave Trade," *Encyclopedia Britannica*, April 6, 2020.

The historical backdrop of the N-word (ni**er) is regularly followed to the Latin word niger, which means black. No matter what its origins, by the early 1800s, it was firmly established as a derogative name. During slavery, the words 'ni**er' and 'Black' were often embedded before a first or given name (e.g., ni**er John or Black John). In the twenty-first century, it remains a principal term of white racism.[117]

Within the Black community in the US, there is disagreement on whether the N-word should be used or not. The first team argues that it must not be used amongst African Americans anymore as it is a form of internal racism. Brando Starkey, the author of *In Defense of Uncle Tom: Why Blacks Must Police Racial Loyalty*, argues that "the internalized oppression revealed itself in various ways. Sometimes the formerly enslaved people clearly, perhaps subconsciously, considered themselves subhuman, just like how their former owners regarded them."[118] Thus, he refrains from using the word like many African Americans today.

The other team uses this word as a form of brotherhood and solidarity. To clarify, "Due to a slight tweak to the spelling and pronunciation of the end of the word, N-word derivatives (ni**a, ni**as, ni**az) have become popular terms of endearment by the descendants of the very people who once

117 Wyman King, et al., "Who has the 'Right' to Use the N-Word? A Survey of Attitudes about the Acceptability of Using the N-Word and its Derivatives," *International Journal of Society, Culture &Language* 6, no.2 (2018): 48.

118 Brando Starkey, "If You Truly Knew What the N-Word Meant to Our Ancestors, You'd Never Use It," *The Undefeated*, May 18, 2017

had to endure the N-word." It can even mean a "friend."[119] Thus, this team believes it is empowering to reclaim a word that has been used as a weapon to persecute and dehumanize them. If they use it, then they can no longer exploit the word to harm African Americans.

African Americans like Sheryll Cashin, author of *Place Not Race*, says she would rather focus her energy on the structural system that creates inequality, poverty, and separate schools rather than on merely a word.[120] Despite it all, it is the choice of African Americans to use or not to use it. It is up to them and them only. It should not be used by anyone outside that community because of its degrading dark history.

BLACKFACE

Blackface is another manifestation of racism in the Arab world.

Historically, the American white working-class started wearing blackface as part of a comedy play called Minstrelsy.

> Thomas Dartmouth Rice, known as the "Father of Minstrelsy," developed the first popularly known blackface character, "Jim Crow," in 1830. By 1845, the popularity of the minstrel had spawned an entertainment subindustry, manufacturing songs and sheet music, makeup, costumes, as well as

119 King, et al., "Who has the 'Right' to Use the N-Word?" 48.

120 "Is There Meaningful Debate to Be Had about Banning the N-Word? | The N-Word Project," *The Washington Post*, accessed September 30, 2020.

a ready set of stereotypes upon which to build new performances.

...

Historian Dale Cockrell once noted that poor and working-class white people who felt "squeezed politically, economically, and socially from the top, but also from the bottom, invented minstrelsy" as a way of expressing the oppression that marked being members of the majority, but outside of the white norm. Minstrelsy, comedic performances of "blackness" by whites in exaggerated costumes and makeup, cannot be separated fully from the racial derision and stereotyping at its core. By distorting the features and culture of African Americans—including their looks, language, dance, deportment, and character—white Americans were able to codify *whiteness* across class and geopolitical lines as its antithesis.[121]

Thus, the misery of African Americans during the Jim Crow law period was turned into comedies undermining their daily sufferings like segregation.

By and large, the Arab world is ignorantly dealing with such issues. When the Black Lives Matter protest took place in the late spring and early summer of 2020, many Arab influences wanted to show solidarity by painting themselves black and posting blackface pictures on their Instagram accounts.

---

121 "Blackface: The Birth of An American Stereotype," *National Museum of African American History and Culture*, November 22, 2017.

Maryam, the influencer, for example, bashed them, saying, "This isn't solidarity. This is racism."[122] Such people completely ignored the fact that Black people went through slavery, humiliation, and segregation. Blackface is insulting, and it is shameful that we still have to explain it to some people today.

If the solidarity of the whole world towards people of color is done right, there is hope for humanity. Tim Wise says, "Only by rebelling against it, and pursuing freedom from the mental straitjacket into which we have been placed as white people by this system, can we hope to regain our full humanity, and be of any use as allies to people of color in their struggle against racism."[123]

XENOPHOBIA, YELLOW FEVER, AND YELLOW PERIL

In California, I remember my Japanese American classmate joking about the coronavirus outbreak to the professor, saying, "Hey, don't worry, I am not that Chinese."

When reports of the first case of coronavirus started in December 2019 in China, many people from all over the world projected prejudice towards Chinese people around them and towards anyone who has Asian features. Merriam-Webster defines xenophobia as the "fear and hatred of strangers or foreigners or of anything that is strange or foreign."[124]

---

122 Maryam Abu Khaled (@maryamabukhaled1), "حبايبي ديرو بالكم بطريقة التضامن لأنو مرات بتكون عكسية ما تكونوا متل هاي الناس كل الناس خير وبركة صباحكم عسل", Instagram photo, June 3, 2020.

123 Tim J. Wise, *Speaking Treason Fluently: Anti-Racist Reflections From an Angry White Male* (Brooklyn: Soft Skull Press, 2008), 250.

124 *Merriam Webster*, s.v. "Xenophobia," accessed September 30, 2020.

Xenophobia is present and destructive in our Palestinian society. One takeaway was how xenophobic some could be. Many Asian people have spoken up about how irritated they were by that.

I have seen xenophobia towards my Korean friends who visit Palestine. Handong Global University (HGU) and BU have a partnership. Every year, the two schools exchange more or less two Palestinian students with two Korean ones. I was one of the students who got to study at HGU in South Korea in Spring 2016. Because of that, I had exposure to another culture that I fell in love with, and I wish those Korean students had the same experience I had as exchange students in Palestine.

Some of those students understood Arabic, some were learning, and some did not know any at all. The last group is the lucky one. They did not comprehend what some Palestinians were saying behind their backs. When I asked one of those Korean friends about it, she said, "They would just shout out from the car 'Asian' or tell me they want to marry me even when they have a beautiful wife." I would classify this under yellow fever. Yellow fever is a sexual fetish for Asian women. Arabs are not the only ones whose sexuality is fantasized. Asian women experience this as well. According to a study on yellow fever by Robin Zheng, Zheng concluded that,

> Even without stereotypical content, racial fetishes depersonalize and Otherize their targets, subjecting them to disproportionate psychological burdens of doubt, suspicion, and insecurity on account of their race. Moreover, regardless of origin, racial fetishes in a racially stratified society are still interpreted and

explained by—and hence express—racially stereo-typic social meanings.[125]

I wish xenophobia and racism towards Asian people ended here, but it does not. I know a Palestinian male who often complains about his eyes, saying, "My eyes look Chinese." This is problematic as Chinese eyes are used in a context that describes them not as beautiful. It becomes offensive to have Chinese-looking eyes, and it should not be the case. Beauty standards differ all around the world, and media platforms cannot keep portraying only white as beautiful.

Therefore, the virus was the veil that blew away and exposed what was slightly hidden. Racism towards Asian people was as clear as glass about to shatter into pieces and wound any-one stepping on its zillion splinters. In Egypt, a video of an Asian man in Cairo went viral after people humiliated him. He was sitting in the back of a taxi. People in the streets were yelling at the taxi driver who was covering his mouth with a tissue, "Why are you keeping him in your taxi? Kick him out!" Because of his race, people assumed that this innocent man had the coronavirus. Everyone was disgusted by him including the taxi driver who eventually kicked him out. The extreme fear of this poor Asian man almost led to his death as he was distraught in the middle of the street with the cars almost hitting him and even touching his body. An incident similar but not as heartbreaking happened in Palestine. Two Asian women shared a video of them talking about what they have experienced in Palestine despite dedicating their time

---

125 Robin Zheng, "Why Yellow Fever Isn't Flattering: A Case Against Racial Fetishes," *Cambridge University Press* 2, no. 3 (October 2016): 400–419.

to volunteer in the Holy Land. They said they were called names like, "Corona! Corona!" by a mother and her child. They also described the fear these women saw in people's eyes when they were in the picture, fearing that these two innocent women had the killer virus.

This type of case is known as the Yellow Peril. "The idea of an awakened China was given a particular meaning by Kaiser Wilhelm II in 1895. Forerunners of Kaiser Wilhelm's version of a 'Yellow Peril' did exist, found in those European fears that arose over the depredations of Genghiz Khan [d. 1227 ce.] who, after 1189, "Made the Mongols the greatest power of central Asia."[126]

The term Yellow Peril originated in a western context toward people of Asian descent. But Arabs can perceive Asian people with superiority as well. According to the theory of Yellow Peril, Asian people were of lower intelligence, uncivilized, and dangerous, leading them to become a threat to a supposedly more civilized nation.[127] It may seem ironic, but in this case, Arabs would be the self-proclaimed civilized nation. However, according to this definition, Asian people are dangerous in 2020. They all have coronavirus because it started in Wuhan, China. Thus, we fear them, for taking something away from us like accusations of stealing all the jobs from white people in the US. This time, taking lives, as wrongly assumed by many Palestinians, Arabs, and almost everyone else.

---

126 Stanford M. Lyman, "The 'Yellow Peril' Mystique: Origins and Vicissitudes of a Racist Discourse," *International Journal of Politics, Culture, and Society* 13, no. 4.

127 "The Theory of Yellow Peril." Study.com. Accessed October 1, 2020.

To wrap this up, racism towards the mongoloid exists in many shapes and forms not only in the western world but in the Arab world and Palestine as well. This depiction occurs through xenophobia, yellow fever, and Yellow Peril that has always been there but was manifested more vigorously after the coronavirus pandemic. Constant unaddressed racism can become normalized, and that is where the biggest problem lies. After 9/11, Arabs, despite their religion, became terrorists. What does that make Asian people after the coronavirus global pandemic? A virus?

INTERNALIZED RACISM

Humans can be internally racist. They might despise the racial aspect of their identity for psychological reasons.

In the US, I have an African American classmate who has only one Black friend amongst the many white friends and her boyfriend. She is okay with them saying the N-word. When her roommate asked her, "Who are you voting for in the presidential election, Trump or Biden?"

The Black girl answered, "I don't know yet. I still can't decide." She believes that providing opportunities for the marginalized Black community is to rob white people of opportunities that should be theirs. Some people refer to this mindset as "reverse racism." However, if white people hold privilege in the system, then people of color can be harmed by that. When one does not have the power, they cannot be racist towards those who hold power. Institutionally, the underprivileged can't harm white people.

Similarly, Palestinians can internalize racism too. Palestinians who have adopted this mindset might choose to support the

Israeli economy, listen to Israeli music, and not boycott Israeli products. Donna Bivens writes,

> As people of color are victimized by racism, we internalize it. That is, we develop ideas, beliefs, actions, and behaviors that support or collude with racism. This internalized racism has its own systemic reality and its own negative consequences in the lives and communities of people of color. More than just a consequence of racism, then, internalized racism is systemic oppression in reaction to racism, that has a life of its own."[128]

Internal racism is dangerous. How does it apply to Palestinians?

I often hear Palestinians hating themselves. They complain about other Arabs with jobs as doctors, nurses, or other jobs predominated by Jewish westerns or Israelis. "An Arab nurse took my soul away today when she drew my blood," an old Palestinian friend once told me. "Since when do they work at Israeli hospitals? It used to be mostly Russian Jews. They were the best." My friend was internalizing racism and reflecting self-hatred. Why would she be not happy that her own people are getting jobs when the unemployment rate is high? Why is she looking down on the Palestinian nurse who is humiliated every day while crossing the checkpoint to work in Israel, where they are underpaid compared to other Israeli workers?

Another major, repetitive example is when Palestinians blast Israeli music in their cars for everyone else to hear. They

---

128 Donna Bivens. "What Is Internalized Racism?" *Flipping the Script: White Privilege and Community Building,*(United States: MP Associates, Inc., 2005), 44.

might think they are the cool kids. However, this reflects their low self-esteem and self-hatred. They are listening to the products of their oppressors and occupiers. They are looking down on themselves and allowing Israel to be the dominant power with its industries. Israel appreciates being in power.

My favorite example of internal Palestinian racism is when a classmate once said, "I'm grateful for Israel. Without it, we wouldn't have malls." Malls in Israeli areas have decent brands, unlike Palestinian malls.

ONE RACE

US civil rights activist Malcolm X once said, "I am not a racist. I am against every form of racism and segregation, every form of discrimination. I believe in human beings, and that all human beings should be respected as such, regardless of their color."[129]

Humanity.

Do we see it?

No

Do we feel it?

No

---

129 Malcolm X and Steve Clark, *By Any Means Necessary* (New York: Pathfinder, 2019), 158.

Why?

Is it because when racism comes in the way, our humanity is distorted?

Or is it because of our humanity, there shouldn't be room for racism?

What if we were all of one race? Would we have that humanity?

When I was a student at Georgetown University as part of the Middle East Partnership Initiative Student Leaders Program (MEPI-SLP), one of our professors' first question was, "How many races do you think there are?"

"Eleven!" someone answered.

"Twenty-one," another student said.

"Over fifty!" A third student increased the number as if he were in an auction. I was expecting the majority to confuse race with ethnicity. This student considered Arab a race rather than an ethnicity, same as Hispanic, Native American, Amazigh, and so on.

In my notebook, I drew a sketch. "Race" was the word at the very top of the page. I dropped three short straight lines putting a word at the lower end of each: *Mongloid, Caucasoid, Negroid.*

Three, I thought to myself, confident that my answer was correct.

"One." I recognized the voice of my friend, coming from the back of the room. "Just one race."

"Ahaaa! We have a romantic poet here," said the professor, expecting such an answer.

One. Just one race. I thought for a second. Even though the romantic poet was scientifically wrong, I liked his answer the best, and I still do.

TAKEAWAYS

- Some Palestinians persecute the small Afro-Palestinian community.

- If you're not Black, don't assert the right to speak the N-word. It's not your word.

- Racism manifests on both personal and systemic levels.

- Blackface has nothing to do with solidarity. It's rooted in a painful past.

- Xenophobia, yellow fever, and Yellow Peril are dangerous and present in Palestine.

- Internal racism can be destructive.

- Individuals shouldn't focus on their different races. They should focus on being humane to each other.

CHAPTER SEVEN

THE CONDEMNED LGBTQIA+ COMMUNITY

"To my siblings—I tried to find redemption and failed, forgive me.

To my friends—the journey was harsh, and I am too weak to resist it, forgive me.

To the world—you were cruel to a great extent, but I forgive."
SARAH HEGAZY

Sarah Hegazy was an outspoken, Egyptian, thirty-year-old LGBTQIA+ rights activist. She ended her life because of the traditional, intolerant attitude towards her sexuality. This is the type of news I wake up to in 2020.

In 2017, Sarah was charged with "promoting sexual deviancy and debauchery." She raised the Rainbow flag in Egypt at a

Mashrou' Leila concert.[130] Thus, the Egyptian government imprisoned her since it refuses to tolerate a nonstraight person. After three months in prison, she was bailed. "She suffered from Post-Traumatic Stress Disorder (PTSD) caused by the humiliation and mistreatment she faced during her imprisonment, which resulted in a failed suicide attempt. She eventually sought asylum in Canada."[131] The success of her subsequent suicide attempt in Canada marks a failure to the people who share her suffering.

In one of her final posts on Instagram, Sarah writes, "The sky is more beautiful than the earth. And I want the sky, not the earth."[132]

After years of torment, bullying, and sexual harassment—including inside the prison—in death, Sarah found sympathy among some Arabs. Some, but not all. Most Arabs didn't sympathize with her at all. They believe that being gay is not religiously acceptable.

SEXUALITIES AND IDENTITIES

I grew up in a fairly conservative Christian family. When I would try to explain to some family members that there is nothing strange about those who are not heterosexual, they perceive me as a lesbian. My relatives would ask, "Why would

---

130 "Egyptian LGBT activist dies by suicide in Canada," *Aljazeera*, June 15, 2020.

131 Ibid.

132 Declan Walsh, "Arrested for Waving Rainbow Flag, a Gay Egyptian Takes Her Life," *The New York Times*, June 15, 2020.

you defend them if you are not one of them?" LGBTQIA+ sounds taboo to them.

LGBTQIA+ stands for Lesbian, Gay, Bisexual, Transgender, Queer or Questioning, Intersex, Asexual, plus other sexualities, identities, nonbinaries, or gender-fluidities.

I can understand why these terms confuse my relatives who believe "sex" and "gender" are interchangeable. They are not. Gender is more inclusive than sex. We have socially perceived sex as a binary term, either male or female. This dismisses the fact that there are nonbinary people in this world like intersex, "A person…born with reproductive or sexual anatomy that doesn't fit the boxes of 'female' or 'male.'"[133] Doctors usually perform surgeries on newborn intersex babies and determine their gender for them. Gender identification can also vary over time. That is gender fluidity. For example, gender fluid people could refer to themselves using he\his pronouns, and the next couple of hours, days, months, years—they could refer to themselves using she\her pronouns or vice versa.

The expectation on the Palestine scale is that one is fully heterosexual. The believers of all humans must be straight tend to attack anyone who does not belong to what these believers refer to as "the norm." What does not fully straight mean? What are the sexualities?

Sexualities can be one or any combination of more than one of the following:

---

133 "What Is Intersex?: Definition of Intersexual," *Planned Parenthood,* accessed October 1, 2020.

- **Heterosexual:** "An adjective used to describe people whose enduring physical, romantic, and/ or emotional attraction is to people of the opposite gender. Also *straight*."[134]

- **Gay/Lesbian:** "The adjective used to describe people whose enduring physical, romantic, and/ or emotional attractions are to people of the same gender (e.g., *gay man*, *gay people*). Sometimes *lesbian* is the preferred term for women."[135]

- **Bisexual:** "A person who has the capacity to form enduring physical, romantic, and/or emotional attractions to those of the same gender or those of another gender. People may experience this attraction in differing ways and degrees over their lifetime. Bisexual people need not have had specific sexual experiences to be bisexual; in fact, they need not have had any sexual experience at all to identify as bisexual,"[136] (as it is, if I may add, with heterosexuals, gays, and lesbians).

- **Asexual:** "People who are asexual may not be interested in sex."[137] Some asexual people feel an emotional connection to others, and some don't.

---

134 Kasandra Brabaw, "Allosexual, Demisexual, Bicurious-& Other Sexualities You Need To Know," *Refinery 29*, accessed October 1, 2020.

135 Ibid.

136 Ibid

137 "Sexual Attraction and Orientation," *Teens Health from Nemours*, accessed October 1, 2020.

- **Pansexual**: "A person who has the capacity to form enduring physical, romantic, or emotional attractions to any person, regardless of gender identity. Pansexual people need not have had specific sexual experiences to be pansexual; in fact, they need not have had any sexual experience at all to identify as pansexual," like any other sexuality.[138]

- **Other sexualities may include:** Allosexual, Aromantic, Androsexual, Demiromantic, Demisexual, Gynesexual, Skolisexual.[139]

Note that the T in LGBTQIA+ —transgender—isn't a sexuality. Transgender is a gender identity for those who feel like their gender does not fit the sex assigned at birth. Some intersex people consider themselves part of the transgender community. The binary gender they are brought up to be is initially not matching their nonbinary sex.

According to a 2018 Ipsos Mori poll, "Sixty-six percent of young people, aged between sixteen and twenty-two, are 'exclusively heterosexual'—the lowest figure of any generation. Among millennials, seventy-one percent say they are exclusively heterosexual, as do eighty-five percent of those in 'Gen X', and eighty-eight percent of baby boomers."[140] Generation X represents people born between 1965–1979, and baby boomers were born between 1944–1964.[141]

---

138 Brabaw, "Allosexual, Demisexual, Bicurious."

139 Ibid

140 Olivia Rudgard, "Only Two-Thirds of Generation Z Identify as 'Exclusively Heterosexual,'" *The Telegraph*, July 5, 2018.

141 "Boomers, Gen X, Gen Y, and Gen Z Explained," *Kasasa*, accessed October 1, 2020.

The list continues to evolve as our understanding of sexuality and gender identity deepens. Accepting those sexualities and identities gives the LGBTQIA+ community hope. It provides them with a reason to live in a world that barely tolerates them. Therefore, I could write pages and pages trying to explain how our sexuality works, but that is not the point. Sometimes, we cannot tell what our sexualities are. One day, you feel you do not belong to the gay community, and the other day you find out that you do, or vice versa. You could have a queer side, and you might not know it. You could be not fully straight, or you might discover you are more than gay. You figure you are either something else or a combination of more than one sexuality. It is hard to be specific about our sexualities. It is a journey. It is a rollercoaster. If we are not on this ride, let those who are enjoy it.

FEMININE DOES NOT MEAN GAY

People often mistake a feminine man for gay and a masculine woman as lesbian. This generalization does not hold true.

Meet Jeries Kitlo, a vibrant, outgoing, twenty-two-year-old man from Bethlehem. Jeries dresses differently but fashionably. He is not tall, his voice is sassy, and he does not fit society's extremely masculine image of the male stereotype. As my friend, he is the life of the party. He is hilarious, fun, and full of character and charisma. I wish more people would take the time to get to know him the way I know him.

Growing up in an all-boy school, Jeries was bullied for his character and for not fitting the male stereotype. He says, "My daily routine at that time was just genuinely hearing sh*t out all day long from everyone. Even on the way home, I used to hear people calling me out, and it was irritating." He explains how many are in consensus that Jeries is "wrong" and unusual. He felt the need to blame someone for the way he was born, and he almost blamed himself. They made it hard for him to accept his own uniqueness. But eventually, he refused to let them take it away from him. Instead, he found that "seed of hope," and it grew in him and kept him going until today.

College created an opportunity for Jeries to set his own boundaries to protect himself from bullying. It was a new page for him, a new beginning, a new life. No one could take that away from him. He says, "I wasn't doing anything morally wrong!" However, the new chapter started to get messy. Finding a job was not easy for him. Usually, Jeries does not meet the expectations of the hirer despite his great achievements and hard work. Jeires applied for the same part-time job at the same restaurant a couple of times. Each time, the manager shut Jeries down. After insisting on getting hired there, Jeries succeeded. He finally got the job. But, one of the employees told him, "We were expecting you to leave the next day. We didn't think you'd handle all the work."

Sometimes, Jeries and those like him go through dark thoughts like questioning their existence. The idea of taking their own lives might seem easier for them. Staying on Earth is to deal with some people's negativity and their projections of unhealthy opinions on subjects like Jeries. Luckily, Jeries is here with us today. Even though his classmates and teachers bullied him in school, he did not feel like he is leaving an impactful legacy behind. Today, he is still working on leaving one.

Manar is the female version of Jeries. Manar is a heterosexual young woman with short messy black hair. She is about the same age as Jeries. Manar usually dresses in flannels and beanies—in summer too. "I've been called gay for most of my life because of my looks. I've also been abused because of the same reason," she says, exhaling the cigarette smoke that slowly draws a picture of grey strings dancing in the blue sky above her.

This leads me to question femininity and masculinity. To dismantle the concept of femininity, femininity is not only about wearing dresses and high heels. It is not about specific gestures and body postures. It is not about having no body hair. It is not about getting attracted to men. It is not about having female genitalia. Femininity could be none of the above. Same with masculinity. It is not about the muscles, facial hair, having a poker face, male genitalia, and so on. Again, masculinity could be none of these. This polarization eliminates everything in between, and there is so much in between.

The amount of hatred, disrespect, and judgment the LGBTQIA+ community receives is unfortunate. Why do we still look down on others by calling them gay? Why do we consider it an insult? Why do we use religion to justify our dehumanization of anyone who is different? Why can't we normalize a feminine male and a masculine woman?

TO BE GAY IN A CONSERVATIVE SOCIETY

In our conservative Palestinian society, being nonstraight comes with horrendous consequences either online or in real life.

Bullying the LGBTQIA+ can be done virtually. Bethlehem University (BU) has a huge Facebook student group. The administrator added me to the group as a first-year student, and I accepted the invitation. As a senior, I have come to regret that decision.

An alumnus and former president of the Student Council posted his observations after paying a visit to the campus. "What the hell happened to this university when I was gone?" he raged. The source of his fury and disgust, as it turned out, was so small that most people would not even notice it. It was an earring. The alumnus had seen a male student wearing an earring. Expressing his nationalistic views on how "glorious" his university was back in his day, the man continued, "How does the university allow this? What world are we living in?" The earring, he assumed, indicated that this student was gay. Such "horrific scenes" were never seen on campus when he was a student.

The comment section had hundreds of comments, and the debate was heated. There was a large group of people defending the earring. The other and much larger group was in support of the former president.

"He isn't hurting anyone," the first team said.

"It doesn't matter. It contradicts our religion," the other team replied, neglecting historical and cultural differences.

The debate lasted for a few hours before the former president of the Student Council deleted the post.

That is one example of cyberbullying. Can you imagine how terrifying real-life bullying would be?

Adel is a gay man bullied on a daily basis for his sexuality. He is a university student who had to leave his village and move to the city of Jerusalem, hoping for a safer future. At first, he feared coming out to his parents. He believed they would kill him because they consider homosexuality "something haram (taboo) in the Quran." He says that when he came out to his parents, "The first thing my father wanted to do was to take me to a psychologist." His parents thought of it as "they were unlucky to have [him]."[142] This made Adel run away and escape the mental pain.

Many consider homosexuality a disease or something chosen, and that is problematic. I remember my friend, Anna Kleiman, shedding tears when a friend told her, "It's your choice not to be straight." To Anna, this was offensive, arguing that belonging to the LGBTQIA+ community is not something one chose. It is how one is born. It is the same reason why homosexuality is not a mental disease.

Many people suffer from mental illness due to traumatic experiences, sometimes even in early childhood. For instance, Abby Stein, a transgender woman who grew up in an ultra-Orthodox Hasidic Jewish community, was traumatized in her childhood. At the age of four, she tried cutting her male organ. As depicted in her autobiography, *Becoming Eve: My Journey from Ultra-Orthodox Rabbi to Transgender Woman*, Stein tells her mother, "I want to be a girl, mommy, and *this* [penis] does not belong on me."[143] Abby prayed every day that God turns

---

142 *Rebel News*, "Shunned: A film about LGBT Palestinians in Israel," July 6, 2015, video, 50:14.

143 Abby Stein, *Becoming Eve: My Journey from Ultra-Orthodox Rabbi to Transgender Woman* (New York: Seal Press, 2019), 54.

her into a girl. She did not know this was possible until she got access to the internet as an adult. Her parents disowned her after the transformation.

Bullying the LGBTQIA+ can also be physical. This community is endangered in Palestine. They find it hard to come out because they have seen their gay friends get beaten. "They are not masculine enough to protect themselves," the bullies would think. Thus, people's intolerance of the LGBTQIA+ community is brutal and unethical. It should be eliminated virtually, psychologically, and physically.

THE DISCOURSE OF "COMING OUT"

Coming out, "the process of being open about one's sexuality and gender,"[144] is a tough process. Coming out is exceptionally difficult in a conservative, Palestinian society. Some manage to come out, and it can be consequential.

On the discourse of coming out, Judith Butler, a gender theorist, asks, "Is the 'subject' who is 'out' free of its subjection and finally in the clear? Or could it be that the subjection that subjectivates the gay or lesbian subject in some ways continues to oppress, or oppresses most insidiously, once 'outness' is claimed?"[145] Butler then elaborates, "If I claim to be a lesbian, I 'come out' only to produce a new and different 'closet.' The 'you' to whom I come out now have access to a

---

144 Mere A brams, "46 Terms That Describe Sexual Attraction, Behavior & Orientation," *Healthline*, December 10, 2019.

145 Judith Butler, "Imitation and Gender Insubordination," *The Lesbian and Gay Studies Reader*, ed. Henry Abelove, Michele Aina Barale, and David M. Halperin (New York: Routledge, 1993), 308–309.

different region of opacity."[146] Her point is that coming out of the closet is not necessarily the end goal achieved. Maybe this closet is in a dim basement with no exit. Thus, even if one comes out, people's homophobia can make it worse than staying inside the closet.

If you are a Palestinian living in occupied Palestine reading this, I want you to think of someone you have perceived as gay. Someone who passed by you the other day. You assumed they were gay for the way they dressed, talked, or walked. If nothing came to your mind, I want you to think of the two guys who were holding each other's hands in in front of you in the street. What were your thoughts on that? What did you say to them? Did you think of stopping them, telling them what is right, explaining to them why it is a sin? Or perhaps, did you spit on them and call them names?

Some can never come out fearing others' homophobia.

TABOOS AND THE ETHICS OF SEXUALITY

Religion does not condemn gay people. Christianity and Islam are not against it. All monotheistic religions focus on worshiping God and loving one another. Do the details matter? Does one need endless rules to be good? It should be clear that people should not harm each other. How come it is okay for you to persecute and project shame towards the LGBTQIA+ community? They are not harming you personally on any level. How does it affect your well-being? If you believe that God does not allow it, then God should take care of it. Not

---

146 Butler, "Imitation and Gender Insubordination," 309.

you. Who are you to decide that the way some were born is wrong? If so, why did God, whose creation is perfect, create nonperfect people?

At college, I took an Islam course. A colleague presented on the acceptance of the LGBTQIA+ community. It made some students uncomfortable. One of these students stood up to her. He tried to convince her that God does not accept this community. "It's haram (a taboo)," he said. The presenter told him, "You're just homophobic." His face turned red. He was boiling with rage. They argued the entire class, each trying to prove their point. In the last five minutes of class, we found out he thought she called him homosexual. Unfortunately, that word is used as an insult in the Palestinian context.

A year later, I had a conversation with my religious friend, Noor. I asked Noor, "Why don't you interact with Anna?" Noor said, "She's not straight." Then, Noor cited the narration of Ibn Abbas, "لَعَنَ رَسُولُ اللَّهِ ﷺ المُتَشبِّهِين مِن الرِّجالِ بالنساءِ، والمُتَشبِّهَات مِن النِّساءِ بالرِّجالِ" meaning, "Allah's Apostle cursed those men who are in the similitude (assume the manners) of women and those women who are in the similitude of men" (Sahih Bukhari, Volume 7, Book 72, Number 773).[147]

Many believe this narration addresses homosexuality, but it addresses cross-dressing. Noor considers herself a stud. She only wears dress shirts, jeans, and sneakers. She also does cross-fit and builds muscles. But isn't that similitude?

---

147 Moin Qazi, *Women In Islam—Exploring New Paradigms* (Triplicane: Notion Press, 2015).

Muslims believe the Quran is the literal word of God, but the narration that Noor cited is not. It is a Hadith, a narrated saying of prophet Muhammad. However, there are cultural and historical differences. What wasn't accepted then can be tolerated now.

As for the Bible, people have intervened in translation. The Bible, written in a period of historical and cultural differences, accepted heterosexuality as the norm. Also, the Bible was written by people who could have added their input in the text. Therefore, humans forced part of their culture into the bible. On the outside, the Bible can seem like a book that bashes the gay community, nonbinary, or gender fluid people. But, when we understand those two gaps, we realize it does not.

A research study proves that homosexuality isn't mentioned in the Bible. The scholar Ed Oxford says,

> I started collecting old Bibles in French, German, Irish, Gaelic, Czechoslovakian, Polish...I had a German friend come back to town, and I asked if he could help me with some passages in one of my German Bibles from the 1800s. So, we went to Leviticus 18:22, and he's translating it for me word for word. In the English where it says, "Man shall not lie with man, for it is an abomination," the German version says, "Man shall not lie with young boys as he does with a woman, for it is an abomination." I said, "What? Are you sure?" He said, "Yes!" Then we went to Leviticus 20:13—same thing, "Young boys." So we went to 1 Corinthians to see how they translated arsenokoitai (original Greek word), and

instead of homosexuals, it said, "Boy molesters will not inherit the kingdom of God."[148]

Thus, the Bible demonizes pedophilia, not Homosexuality. Some cultures refused to accept the LGBTQIA+ for the longest time. God did not necessarily say homosexuality is not accepted. Instead, people had input based on their comprehension of what is culturally accepted and what is not.

Furthermore, a famous Christian argument I have heard over and over again is that we should love our bodies the way they are without making any adjustments. These religious people apply this claim to transgender women and men or intersex people with nonbinary genitalia. However, if these Christians sincerely believed in God and his perfect creation, why did God create some imperfectly in wrong bodies that make them unhappy? Why do they pray to God to bless them with the bodies they would be satisfied with? Why did they get unlucky?

Lastly, many religious people argue that homosexuality is not accepted because it goes against nature in the sense of conceiving. They claim that it is impossible for a homosexual couple to conceive children and continue the cycle of life. This is one of the main arguments used against the marriage of the same gender.

In our scientifically and technologically advanced world, same-gender couples can have a child. Even if the child does

---

148 The Forge Online, "Has 'Homosexual' Always Been in the Bible?" *United Methodist Insight*, October 14, 2019.

not have both of the parents' DNA, it can be the product of a parent's egg or sperm. If that is too expensive, adoption is always another option. Many children wish to be adopted. There are many children in this world in need of shelter and caring parents, straight or nonstraight. Moreover, today, two eggs can make a female baby because XX and XX chromosomes produce an XX chromosome.[149]

Some argue it could be unhealthy for the children to grow up with same-sex parents. However, research shows that,

> Although most children of same-sex couples are biological children of one of the parents, a growing number are the result of donor insemination, surrogacy, foster care, and adoption. Most research studies show that children with two moms or two dads fare just as well as children with heterosexual parents.[150]

Yes, having same-gender parents is not unhealthy, as many try to claim. They want to perceive it as unhealthy. And why bring more children to this world? The world is already overwhelmed with its various problems. I wish I did not have to use the famine argument, but there are a large number of children suffering from famine, like in Yemen. Aside from famine, would you want to bring children to the world who may not accept and possibly bully your different children?

---

149 "New Fertility Procedure Allows 2 Women to Carry Same Baby, Presents New Choices for Same-Sex Couples," ABC7 San Francisco, October 29, 2018.

150 "Same Sex Parents and Their Children," American Association for Marriage and Family Therapy, accessed October 1, 2020.

To provide a better and more accepting environment for our children, we should accept those who are different.

TAKEAWAYS

- Sex is not necessarily binary, or male and female.

- We should make room in society for the exploration of one's sexuality.

- We do not choose our sexual orientation. We are born with it.

- We perceive femininity and masculinity in a stereotypical way.

- Bullying can take many forms: virtual, physical, emotional, mental, and sexual.

- Coming out is not the end of the journey. It is the beginning of a new one.

- Religious dogma does not condemn homosexuality. Individuals do.

PART III

MAKING CHANGE

CHAPTER EIGHT

CHANGE ON A GLOBAL LEVEL: THE ERADICATION OF CAPITALISM

———

"My idea is to live in a society where some invisible alienated machinery takes care of things, so I can do whatever I want: watch movies, read and write philosophical books and so on."

SLAVOJ ŽIŽEK[151]

In America, "[The] richest one percent now own half the value of the US stock market. The richest ten percent own ninety-two percent. So when Trump says the stock market is the economy, know who he's really talking about."[152]

---

151 *Big Think*, "Slavoj Žižek: Democracy and Capitalism Are Destined to Split Up," January 7, 2015, video, 17:19.

152 Robert Reich (@RBReich), "Your reminder that America's richest 1 percent now own half the value of the US stock market," Twitter, July 5, 2020, 4:44 p.m.

This is the result of capitalism and our acceptance of this corrupt system.

When talking about class struggle, it would make sense to talk about the discrimination of Palestinians against those who do not own much. Poor people suffer in many other parts of the world too. In the case of class struggle, discrimination does not come from the people. It comes from the capitalistic system that exploits the poor. I believed I should talk about the Palestinian gaze towards people who live in villages in poor conditions. About how we can use offending slurs referring to them like, "You look like a Fallah(a) (peasant)." Soon, I realized the problem is much deeper than that, and it starts with the question: why do we have poor people in the first place?

Individuals can and should make a change on a personal level, but real, lasting change can only come when individuals demand change on a systemic level. Changes at this scale can seem unimaginable. The philosopher Slavoj Žižek says,

> Think about the strangeness of today's situation. Thirty, forty years ago, we were still debating about what the future will be: communist, fascist, capitalist, whatever. Today, nobody even debates these issues. We all silently accept global capitalism is here to stay. On the other hand, we are obsessed with cosmic catastrophes: the whole life on earth disintegrating, because of some virus, an asteroid hitting the earth, and so on. So the paradox is that it's much easier to imagine the end of all life on

earth than a much more modest radical change
in capitalism.[153]

KARL MARX'S ESTRANGEMENT OF WORKERS
IN THE PALESTINIAN CONTEXT

Humans are not born to work. Humans are born to live and be.

According to Slavoj Žižek, the irresolvable deadlock is the
reality of class struggle. Jamil Khader explains, "In Lacanian
terms, the deadlock is the impossible traumatic real of the
class struggle that is repressed in the formal structure of
architectural design through the workings of official ideology,
and the wide range of architectural designs are Imaginary
and Symbolic solutions that aim to cover up this void which
makes reality incomplete, but fail to do so."[154]

Nowadays, people work to survive, nationally and globally. We
see that in many places due to the polarization of the rich and
poor and the unfair distribution of wealth, in Marxist terms.

Karl Marx maintains that there are "two classes," the bourgeoisie who make capital, and the laborers who do the work.[155]
The rich become richer, and the poor become poorer. According to Marx,

---

153 Speculative Realism, "Žižek! [Full Movie | 2005]," September 18, 2019,
     video, 55:46.

154 Jamil Khader, "Architectural Parallax, Neoliberal Politics and
     the Universality of the Palestinian Struggle: Banksy's Walled Off
     Hotel," *European Journal of Cultural Studies* 23, no. 3 (2020): 474–94.

155 Karl Marx, and Friedrich Engels, "Economic and Philosophic
     Manuscripts of 1844," 1956, 69.

The more the worker produces, the less he has to consume; the more values he creates, the more valueless, the more unworthy he becomes; the better formed his product, the more deformed becomes the worker; the more civilized his object, the more barbarous becomes the worker, the mightier labor becomes, the more powerless becomes the worker; the more ingenious labor becomes, the duller becomes the worker and the more he becomes nature's bondsman.[156]

In his *Estranged Labor*, Marx discusses the four types of alienation.

1. The alienation of the worker from "the product of labor."[157]

2. The alienation of the worker from the "labor process."[158]

3. The alienation of the worker from their "species-being."[159]

4. The alienation of "man from man."[160]

The four types of estrangement above apply to the local Palestinian level due to capitalism and the Israeli occupation. Many Palestinians from the West Bank are given permits and cross the Israeli checkpoints almost every day to work

---

156 Marx and Engels, "Economic and Philosophic Manuscripts of 1844," 73.

157 Marx and Engels, "Economic and Philosophic Manuscripts of 1844," 75.

158 Ibid.

159 Ibid.

160 Marx and Engels, "Economic and Philosophic Manuscripts of 1844," 78.

in construction in Israel and its settlements. These laborers are a modern-day example of the four types of estrangement that Marx wished to eliminate in the nineteenth century.

1. **Palestinians are estranged from the fruits of their labor.** Let us focus on the example of construction in Israel. Palestinians build in Israel, including its settlements that are branching out in the West Bank. Palestinian workers will never live in those buildings because of both capitalism and colonialism. Why capitalism? "The more objects the workers produce, the fewer can he possess, and the more [they] fall under the domination of his product, capital."[161] Why the occupation? Israel prohibits Palestinians born in the West Bank and Gaza to live in the Israeli parts.

2. **Palestinians are alienated from the means of production.** They have no control over their "own activity."[162] This includes wages. "Israeli employers in the settlements were obliged to pay their Palestinian workers the minimum wage paid in Israel according to a military order from 1982."[163] They cannot negotiate anything with their Israeli employers. They work to survive. They do not choose when to work, how to work, and what to make.

---

161 Marx and Engels, "Economic and Philosophic Manuscripts of 1844," 71.

162 Marx and Engels, "Economic and Philosophic Manuscripts of 1844," 75.

163 Noga Kadman, "Employment of Palestinians in Israel and the Settlements: Restrictive Policies and Abuse of Rights," *Kav LaOved*, 2012. *https://palestinakomiteen.no/wp-content/uploads/2013/05/employment-of-palestinians-in-Israel.pdf*

3. **Palestinian workers are estranged from their own species-being.** We should not work to live. We should live. Humans are conscious of their existence. But capitalism—and in the Palestinian case, the occupation too—prevents them from existing humanely. For example, Israeli capitalism prevents them from having a social life. One weekend, I recall seeing many Palestinian workers in the hot summer of 2020 in the shadow of the coronavirus pandemic carrying their clothes in bags at the checkpoint. They were entering Bethlehem after spending the week in Jerusalem because it was safer for everyone to do it that way. Hence, they had no access to interacting with their families back home. These workers sacrifice their own time to provide a decent life for their families.

4. **Palestinian workers are alienated from each other.** They go to work, do their job under the burning sun, take the money they need to sustain their families, and leave. The labor process does not give them the time to socially interact with other laborers. It would cost employers money. In a capitalistic society, it is all about the money and exploitation.

Undocumented Mexican immigrants in the US, who cannot legally obtain employment, share similarities with Palestinian workers. When they find employers willing to hire them without proper documentation, they may be able to provide for their families, but they forfeit the protections afforded to American workers. To speak out against unfair wages or unsafe working conditions would be to risk deportation. Thus, the circumstances become primed for abuse and exploitation. The workers suffer from Marx's four types of estrangement, but why does this alienation still take place today? Marx would say it happens because people are brainwashed to think capitalism is needed, whether it is fair to everyone or not. Capitalism exploits workers, and billionaires become richer.

GLOBAL CAPITALISM AND FREE WILL

"No one ever makes a billion dollars," says Alexandria Ocasio-Cortez, a member of the US House of Representatives. "You *take* a billion dollars."[164]

Global capitalism is "a qualitatively new stage in the open-ended evolution of capitalism characterized by the rise of transnational capital, a transnational capitalist class, and a transnational state."[165]

Freedom is essential. In a world focused on capital, attaining freedom seems impossible. Palestinians are aware of their unfreedom. Others, however, are not. In an interview, Žižek says that the most "dangerous unfreedom" is the one unaware of itself.[166] He explains that *unfreedom* takes place when our lives are controlled and regulated without the people's awareness of it.[167] "The paradox I see is that we're treated more and more like free subjects: free choice, everything depends on us...But at the same time, we are more and more

---

164 NowThis News, "AOC Calls Out Billionaires at MLK Day Event," January 24, 2020, video, 4:22.

165 William I Robinson, "Global Capitalism: Crisis of Humanity and the Specter of 21st Century Fascism," *The World Financial Review*, May 27, 2014.

166 Big Think, ""Slavoj Žižek."

167 Ibid.

determined by economic and even military processes that are impenetrable. Agency is taken from us."[168]

Real freedom, to Žižek, is the ability to do whatever we want in life without having to worry about anything else. Machines do it for us. It is a notion that some find incomprehensible. As my friend pointed out, "Who will make the robots? And when they do, don't you think they deserve to earn what they've worked for?"

In Marx's ideal world, the issue is not who makes the robots or who capitalizes on them. Instead, the issue is that those who make them do so for fun. Those who share their talents with the world do so for humanitarian reasons. This way, Marxism does not kill our creativity; it utilizes our talents.

If I could live my life the way Žižek describes it, I would travel and experience different cultures. But that is not cheap in a global capitalist society. It is not simple either. Ironically, global capitalism allows money to flow internationally with a click, but not the people. To travel between countries, we must first apply for visas and get accepted. Countries must issue visas because nations have borders. The borders prevent us from internationalism, from functioning as a universal, globalized world.

CAPITALISM AND RELIGION

"Why has religion, more so than politics or law, been able to capitalize on the process of globalization?" asks Miguel

---

168 *Dictionary.com*, s.v. "Femicide," accessed October 4, 2020.

Vatter in *Crediting God: Sovereignty and Religion in the Age of Global Capitalism.*[169]

On the institutional level, religious institutions can be corrupt. In the Church, for example, those at the top have the power. If the Church depends on donations, many a time, we hear of religious leaders using the church funds for their benefit. It gets bigger than that.

Not separating between religion and politics is one of the main reasons why such religious countries are capitalistic. "The question of politics in Judaism returned to the forefront following the creation of the State of Israel," writes Shmuel Trigano.[170] It is unlikely that the State of Israel is formed without the religious argument. According to the 2020 index, Israel's economy ranks twenty-sixth worldwide.[171] It is part of the Israeli culture that is derived from religion to become successful and make money. The Israeli serial entrepreneur Yossi Vardi says that every founder needs a Jewish mother, for whom no achievement is good enough.[172] Because they have guaranteed a state, they cannot help losing it. They have to work hard to maintain. Sometimes, that maintenance comes from exploiting Palestinians and crushing them just like the bourgeoisie did to the laborers.

---

169 Miguel Vatter, ed. *Crediting God: Sovereignty and Religion in the Age of Global Capitalism*. (New York: Fordham University Press, 2011), 2.

170 Vatter, *Crediting God*

171 2020 Index of Economic Freedom, "Israel," accessed October 17, 2020

172 Mastersofscale, "The Next Silicon Valley: Linda Rottenberg on Masters of Scale," January 30, 2020.

America is a capitalist country that incorporates Christianity. "In the United States, Christianity might be capitalism's most impressive conscription so far."[173] The US is "beset by a curious interlude of manufactured hypercapitalist Christianity."[174] According to the 2019 data from the US Census Bureau, "about one in eight Americans still live below the poverty line."[175] The rich become richer, and the poor become poorer. Capitalism gives power. Through relations with other capitalist countries, they exploit powerless countries. Take for example, the US invasion of Iraq. While the authentic motivation for the war continues to be a debate, I believe the invasion was motivated primarily by oil. As a Middle Easterner, I cannot be persuaded that the war benefitted the people of Iraq.

As for Palestine, when Israel forms relations with capitalist countries, I see them exploiting Palestinians more and more. The US provides the aid and assistance needed to annex more Palestinian land. It also makes Jerusalem the capital of Israel. It formalizes the exploitation.

Saudi Arabia, also a capitalistic country, incorporates Islam in the rulings of the Kingdom. It pours "billions of petrodollars into development projects and private industry...'In Saudi Arabia, we want to do everything very quickly,' said Hussein A. Sijini, Assistant Deputy Minister of Planning."[176]

---

173 Elizabeth Bruenig, "Gods and Profits," *The New Republic*, April 20, 2015.

174 Ibid.

175 Pam Fessler, "US Census Bureau Reports Poverty Rate Down, But Millions Still Poor," NPR, September 10, 2019.

176 Douglas Martin, "Saudi Arabia's New Capitalism," The New York Times, February 21, 1982.

Saudi Arabia has the second-largest oil reserve, and "its strategic location all play a role in the long-standing bilateral relationship between the Kingdom and the United States."[177] Countries wise, to the proverb "the enemy of my enemy is my friend," I say, *The friend of my enemy is my enemy.* The US's relation with Israel indirectly exploits Palestinians and increases the capital of Israel, the US, and Saudi Arabia. Thus, religion must not overlap with the state policies as it exploits those with no power.

GLOBAL CAPITALISM AND WOMEN

Global capitalism takes advantage of women through femicide and sex trafficking.

Capitalism creates femicide, the killing of a woman, or a girl by a male domestic partner or member of the family on account of her gender.[178] The murder of Israa Ghrayyeb by her male family members inspired me to write this book. The patriarchal society's justification of her murder as an honor killing called me to act. Infamous serial killer Ted Bundy similarly used morality as justification for his horrific actions, maintaining that to kill a prostitute—unlike murdering a child—benefits society. Yet, there is no moral justification for killing. Even as a daughter, Israa's family holds no power to choose her death for her. As Jubran Khalil Jubran writes, "Your children

---

177 US Department of State, "US Relations With Saudi Arabia," November 26, 2019.

178 Tedbundystuff, "Ted Bundy Documentary - Death Row Tapes (Full)," February 21, 2017, video, 43:58.

are not your children. They are the sons and daughter of life's longing for itself."[179]

In feminist terms, the male forcefully shows he has control over women. He believes his gender hold power in intra-family murder. The power usually comes from the father, the husband, or the brother being the main source of income in the house. It involves social capitalism. Men work outside while women work inside the house.

As for the Marxist point of view, Jamil Khader explains how global capitalism relates to femicide. He argues, "Since the capitalist mode of production constitutes the totality of social relations today, the critique of the culturalization of political problems should, therefore, be radicalized. After all, global capitalism ultimately generates the contradictions and conditions within which these heinous crimes are perpetrated."[180]

He further clarifies,

> Making global capitalism visible locates intra-family femicide within the material realities of economic globalization. It can also reveal the extent to which global capitalism uses colonialism and patriarchy to reproduce, and at the same time conceal, the hegemony of the global economic order. Situating intra-family femicide within the global economy and the feminization of poverty in the new world

---

179 Poets.org, "On Children by Kahlil Gibran - Poems | Academy of American Poets," accessed October 4, 2020.

180 Jamil Khader, "The Invisible Link: Honor Killing and Global Capitalism," *Jadaliyya* 3, no.1 (January 2013).

order makes it possible to interrogate the ubiquity of misogynistic violence in patriarchal cultures not only in Arab countries but also around the world. In its global expansion to the remote corners of the world in search of new markets and cheaper sources of labor, the neoliberal ideology of economic globalization recodes women's labor and redefines the parameters of their mobility. Consequently, traditional gender formations themselves get disrupted as Western notions of freedom and the division of labor are negotiated and appropriated. This cultural disruption happens in complete disproportion to the deteriorating economic conditions among Palestinians. The exclusion of Palestinians from Israel's capitalist economy, which is now increasingly outsourced to migrant workers from around the world, is happening now more than ever. And the crisis of tradition and gender, in turn, is violently acted out on women's bodies.[181]

Palestinian women should not be sick of their culture. They should be sick of capitalism. Culture does not commodify women's bodies. Culture does not justify killing women. Culture does not exploit us. Patriarchy does not take advantage of women as much as global capitalism does.

Global capitalism also plays a role in sex trafficking. This usually starts at a small and local level, prostitution. On an evident national level, people usually despise the idea of sex workers, and this is where the male gaze plays a huge role.

---

181 Ibid.

Many men hate the idea sex workers. Their gaze judges these women. Yet, many still find refuge in them. These women are looked down upon because they say, "I can do what I want with my body, and no one can tell me otherwise." Almost everyone tells them otherwise. Yet, objectifying women benefits global capitalism.

Prostitution is an opportunity for some capitalists. It becomes a means for their exploitation. Khader addresses this by claiming, "According to the capitalist logic of surplus-value, covering up these heinous crimes is more profitable than investigating them. Hence, it becomes generally acceptable that these women are exploited as workers and as women before they are marked for disposal."[182]

In the case of the wealthy businessman, Jeffrey Epstein, it started with molesting these underage girls to satisfy his pedophilia and paraphilia using his money and power.[183] Later on, it turned into turning his desire to possessing them and productizing them in a business of international sex trafficking. "Typically, offenders purchase a beautiful young girl for $1,000 in a Third World country and bring her to the United States, prostitute her, and make the money back in two days."[184] It is pure evil, and capitalism justifies it. When the global system is capitalist, it becomes almost impossible to stop.

---

182 Ibid.

183 *Jeffrey Epstein: Filthy Rich*, directed by Lisa Bryant, aired May 27, 2020, on Netflix.

184 Sgt. Ana Andino, "Latest Lesson in Human Trafficking Features More than Just Sex Slaves; How about Cases of Organ Harvesting," Houston Police Officers' Union, accessed October 26, 2020.

Thus, it is time to stop blaming things on culture and focus on eliminating global capitalism.

CAPITALISM AND DISCRIMINATION

"The world is laughing at us," an American teacher told one of her students in my presence after the first 2020 presidential debate between President Donald Trump and Joe Biden.

Indeed.

We should accept a universal system that cares about the commons and the people, especially the marginalized like the African American community or the LGBTQIA+. The more extreme the bias, the higher the chance of change.

Žižek says, "That cost me dearly in my popularity when I said I'd have voted for Trump. I'm not crazy. Trump is a nightmare. But I claim there would be no #MeToo and no Bernie Sanders without Trump. There's the idea that sometimes a more radical enemy opens up more space for us, and something new might emerge from that. It's a desperate optimism."[185]

Similarly, on June 6, 2020, Black Lives Matter protests peaked "when half a million people turned out in nearly 550 places across the United States. That was a single day."[186] Such protests will continue until white cops stop killing unarmed Black

---

185 New Internationalist, "The Interview: Slavoj Žižek," May 3, 2019.

186 Larry Buchanan, Quoctrung Bui, and Jugal K. Patel, "Black Lives Matter May Be the Largest Movement in US History," *The New York Times*, July 3, 2020.

people with impunity. There wouldn't be pride parades in Jerusalem if it wasn't for the persecution of the gay community.

Trump started as an entrepreneur. He does not care about the wealth of commoners. He cares about his own. He would crush anyone in his way if that increased his power. This includes crushing those he considers of the inferior race or nonstraight. He is racist, and his many tweets prove it. One example is calling African Americans "THUGS."[187] His refusal to denounce white supremacy in the first debate proves it.

COMMUNITY ORGANIZING

It's very difficult to change the system globally. But, if we move a step lower, we can make a change on the grassroots level. Community organizing is one example. Sthela Holly Hanitrinirina, the founder of Gender Justice for Madagascar, describes community organizing as "a way to respond and tackle issues occurring on a local, national and international level. When a community comes together, they are coming together as a group with shared ideas, cultures, and understanding of the reality of the community."

Thus, community organizing allows the community to make a change according to the community's needs. It brings them to the local authority. It allows them to advocate for policymaking. Eventually, it brings change on the national level. "The power of community organizing is its ability to use everyone

---

187 Isobel Asher Hamilton, "Twitter Slapped a 'Glorifying Violence' Label on a Trump Tweet That Threatened George Floyd Protesters in Minneapolis with Getting Shot," Business Insider, May 29, 2020.

in the community no matter of gender, social-economic status, educational level," Sthela adds. "It is fully focusing on gathering all the local skills to better the community."

Change starts small.

TAKEAWAYS

- We have accepted capitalism that creates class struggle.

- Palestinian workers in Israel are estranged and exploited by Israeli capitalism.

- Capitalism deprives us of our freedom.

- Many of the capitalistic countries do not separate religion and politics.

- Global capitalism kills women.

- Capitalism discriminates.

- Universality is the key to change.

- Community Organizing is a small step to a bigger change.

CHAPTER NINE

MAKING CHANGE ON THE PERSONAL LEVEL

———

"Whether you feel like you can or can't, you could or you should."[188]

JOSEPH R. CAMPBELL

I've been spotlighting Palestine's dirt because I want to clean it up. I do not want to see it anymore.

I reject my friends' suffering.

I refuse to watch my children and their children endure the struggles I have endured.

When I address Palestinians, I propose changes to foster a more tolerant environment.

---

188 *TEDx Talks,* "Five steps to becoming an advocate," January 30, 2018, Video, 7:00.

While this chapter evolves around making the necessary change in Palestine, it is valid to emphasize that despite all the discrimination in the Holy Land, some aspects remain positive.

In my travels, I am an ambassador of the Palestinian youth. I usually reflect a positive image. A real image. A non-orientalist image. I challenge stereotypes. I create hope. But, I also need to see that hope within Palestine.

As Palestinians, we have romanticized any fight other than our fight for freedom. It is time to change that. We should fight for those persecuted for their gender, race, color, class, and anything that makes them different.

Thus, despite the unseen within my country that is now seen, the unspoken that is now spoken, the harshness, the discrimination, and the prejudice, the Palestinian culture shines in its own ways as well. Still, we can, and we should make a change, at least on a personal level.

APPRECIATING PALESTINIAN CULTURE

Different cultures fascinate me, but I have always found problematic aspects of my culture. In my culture, patriarchy is dominant, and women are restricted. In my culture, religion has the final say. Yet, in my culture, there are several positive traits. It is that needle in a haystack. It is the hope for a better future. So, what are these positive traits?

To begin with, homelessness is not a huge issue for Palestinians despite the low GDP of the country. "Restrictions on the movement of people and goods, and the separation of the Palestinian economy from international markets (Israel controls all Palestinian borders) are largely responsible for the West Bank's low GDP."[189]

Palestinians like taking care of each other. Homelessness is not culturally acceptable in Palestine. It is considered taboo for someone not to have a home. People would offer their own homes to help someone in need of one. For example, family members can offer help and support. In 2016, "in the West Bank [Israeli authorities] demolished 274 residential buildings and 372 non-residential buildings. Those lucky enough to have family able to take them in find some shelter."[190] In the case of a mental health disorder, a psychiatric hospital would take them in. Also, some nonprofits offer a place to stay depending on their age group. This includes family-oriented orphanages like SOS Children's Village or shelters for the elderly. It is a human right to have a shelter.

Another aspect I appreciate about my culture is hospitality. It is that one thing I miss when I am away from home. As a student studying in Southern California, where wildfires are typical, my Syrian and Vietnamese friends and I evacuated to an American friend's household. In our cultures, Palestinian, Syrian, and Vietnamese, impolite guests ask for food. Rather, it is anticipated that the host offers the food.

"I'm starving," says Rama, my Syrian friend, the day after the evacuation. "We haven't eaten anything since yesterday!"

---

189 Kyrie Melnyck, "Homelessness in Israel/Palestine," *Homeless Entrepreneur*, February 22, 2017.

190 Ibid.

"I'm starving too! But I grabbed this Starbucks bagel from my fridge right before we left," I say.

"OMG! Food!" She jumps. "Oh." She stops for a couple of seconds and complains after holding it, "It's stone hard! I am not eating that!" Her shrugged shoulders relax with her sigh of disappointment. We kept on starving.

Christopher Kai, the CEO of the Mathem Group, interviewed me as an entrepreneur for his Gifter's Podcast. In the interview, he mentioned how Palestinians are "so kind, and so giving, and so generous," making his trip to Ramallah, Palestine, one of the most powerful, "memorable, and meaningful trips."[191]

Thus, the above examples show that my culture has some good aspects that should be celebrated. Most of the Arabs I interact with outside Palestine emphasize how much they miss the empathy, hospitality, food, dance, and music of their home countries.

HOW CAN YOU MAKE A CHANGE?

Despite the caring and hospitable Palestinian culture, problematic aspects remain part of our society, like the marginalization of the Other, minorities, or those who do not fit in. This section shows how change can be made on a personal level regardless of the type of change needed or the country of your origin.

---

191 Christopher Kai, "Tamar Haddad," May 7, 2019, *Anchor*, podcast, episode 448, 9:54.

In the pages of people I follow on my social media, I read about people persecuted or killed every day for accepting their differences and for insisting that there is nothing wrong with their choices or the way they were born. Sometimes, they even choose to take their own lives like Sarah Hejazi, who was not accepted for her sexuality. Every time such posts bothered me—a lot. However, from my personal experience, it becomes even more shocking when someone you know dies because they refused to fit into the consensus of a norm.

When my friend Israa Ghrayeb was murdered by her three male family members, I could not believe it. What seemed to be only portrayed in social media is not as distant as I thought it would be. The pictures came to life. The horror is experienced, especially that this time it is a picture of someone I knew and interacted with. How could she be so close, yet so far in a way? I had no idea what she was going through, and I could not predict she will die in an honor killing for a trifle. There was nothing I could do then, but there is something I can do now, and so can you.

Even though I have come to realize I would probably die before seeing this change, that I would barely make any difference, it is still worth it to have a positive impact in my community. Life would be much easier if we embraced our differences. I hope the theoretical readings of the stories mentioned in this book helped you accept diversity more. So, the next step becomes, what can we do to help those who are surviving today but living in agony?

Keep in mind activism methods that make a change differ from a culture to another. Petitions work in the US, for example, but are not effective in Palestine. However, hunger strikes are popular in Palestine. Even the success chance of protests differs from a place to another. It is all about the constant process of trial and error despite its consequences. It sounds like it is highly influenced by Karl Marx and Vladimir Lenin, who called for a revolution—one more radical than the other.

PAY IT FORWARD

One simple rule: When you receive help, give others help too. The more you give, the better.

Pay It Forward is a 2000 movie that explains the Pay It Forward tree to seventh graders.[192] A recipient of a favor should help three people, and it has to be a favor that recipients cannot do themselves. Then, the new recipients pay it forward and help another three. And the tree grows bigger and bigger.

RANDOM ACTS OF KINDNESS

According to Adam Grant in his bestseller book, *Give and Take*, people are classified into three main categories:

1. **Takers** prefer getting rather than giving. They believe that for them to win, others must lose.

2. **Givers** would rather give than receive. Helping others is more important than their personal costs.

3. **Matchers** balance taking and giving.[193]

---

192 "Pay It Forward," *Bel-Air Entertainment*, directed by Mimi Leder (CA: Warner Bros. Pictures, 2000), DVD.

193 Adam Grant, *Give and Take: a Revolutionary Approach to Success* (London: Weidenfeld & Nicolson, 2014).

Grant explains that givers succeed in life.

But, there can also be a darker side to giving. It is called the White Savior Industrial Complex (WSIC).

Teju Cole once tweeted, "The white savior supports brutal policies in the morning, founds charities in the afternoon, and receives awards in the evening."[194] Cole continues, "The White Savior Industrial Complex is not about justice. It's about having a big emotional experience that validates privilege."[195]

In a Clinton Global Initiative University (CGI U) webinar, the social justice advocate, Ryan Ubuntu Olson, questioned the dark history of white people like himself. He says that historically, his people colonized others throughout the world. Then, the same white people helped those they colonized. But in many cases, that assistance would not have been necessary in the first place if it wasn't for their exploitation. The webinar facilitator, Brittany A. Aronson, supported this, saying, "Ultimately, people are rewarded from saving those less fortunate, and are able to completely disregard the policies they have supported that have created and maintained systems of oppression."[196] Many of those westerners who support Palestinians suffer from the white

---

194 Teju Cole, "The White-Savior Industrial Complex," *The Atlantic*, January 11, 2013).

195 Ibid.

196 Brittany A. Aronson, "The White Savior Industrial Complex: A Cultural Studies Analysis of a Teacher Educator, Savior Film, and Future Teachers," *Journal of Critical Thought and Praxis* 6, no.3 (2017): 36–54.

savior complex.[197] Olivia also admitted that when she first came to Palestine as a volunteer from the Netherlands, she suffered from the complex too. It made her feel so good to help others in need.

Whatever the motivation of the giver or the magnitude of the gift, there is power in giving. Even a small gesture or even a few words can have a great effect on someone's life.

Ernest grew up modestly in a family of eight children in Indiana. In his early sixties, he tells me, "My family did not value schooling or education. We were poor, and no one in my family had ever graduated high school." One morning, at the age of seven, he was late for school. He was dallying as he made his way. He passed by an elderly man, working hard, manually patching a pothole in the road.

The elderly man stopped his work. In a gentle, calm voice, he asked young Ernest, "Aren't you late for school?"

"Yes!" surprised and a little stunned, Ernest answered.

"I wasn't able to go to school when I was young. I was always late. Dallying. Just like you now." The man glanced at one of his tools. "That's why I have to do this kind of work to make a living. You hurry on now and study hard so you won't have to do this kind of work when you are old like me."

Ernest says, "To this day, I can still see him in his tattered jeans and sweat-stained t-shirt, working alone in the morning

---

197 "The American White Savior Complex," Tablet Magazine, June 6, 2019.

sun from a rundown flatbed truck. He was kind; he spoke softly and offered only encouraging words."

The elderly man was unaware of the change his few words had on Ernest's life. He graduated high school, college, and eventually graduate school. "When things got tough, and I wanted to quit, it wasn't my parents or counselors or any of my teachers that motivated me to value and treasure my education," Ernest says. "It was a random act of kindness from a stranger."

ADVOCATE
Be a vocal activist, and let others follow your example.

Joseph R. Campbell is the co-creator of the award-winning independent movie *Doubting Thomas*. In a 2017 TEDx Talk, he argues, "Advocacy by the core is a deeply embedded sense of purpose."[198] This statement resonates with me, as one who has struggled to find meaning in life and found it in advocacy.

How do we become advocates? Campbell says that to pay it forward through advocacy, we must:

1. Lock down our motivation

2. Establish our role models

3. Understand our historical context

---

198 *TEDx Talks*, "Five steps to becoming an advocate."

4. Focus

5. Find our way forward[199]

The activist Milka Derisma once told me, "Don't be afraid to be disruptive to raise awareness."

TRAVEL

When was the first time you traveled alone? For me, it was a trip to Germany at the age of fifteen. Every year, the German Academic Exchange Service (DAAD) covers the costs of hundreds of high schoolers from all over the world to learn German through experiencing Germany for one month. *Ja, ich spreche Deautsch.*

That trip opened a whole new gateway, and I could not wait to explore it. My upbringing was very conservative, but when I traveled, I encountered different people, fascinating cultures, and interesting lifestyles. That first taste of travel occurred at an age when my world view was beginning to take shape. Exposure to diverse people, places, and adventures paved the path to seeking similar experiences. And the goal is to develop a more tolerant mentality today. The list of names appearing in this book's Acknowledgments represents twenty-seven different countries, each of them home to a friend who believed in the importance of diversity and wanted to help amplify the book's message.

Now, you might say, "Well, I'm not as lucky to be part of such exchange programs." You can also say, "Traveling is not for everyone. It's expensive." Wrong.

---

199 Ibid.

By the time Priyanka Surio was twenty-nine, she had visited forty countries. Now a travel expert and author of *Third Culture Kids of the World: Exploring Sustainable Travel Mindsets*, Priyanka teaches new adventurers how to travel more sustainably, which goes hand in hand with less expensive travel.

"Traveling costs usually consist of three main things," she says. "Accommodations, transportation, and food...the more open-minded we are to the possibilities of needing less, the more budget-friendly we become."

To keep accommodations budget-friendly, Priyanka suggests camping, staying in an Airbnb or hostel, or—for the truly adventurous—making new friends and staying as guests in their homes for free. As for flight reservations, she says to do your research and check multiple flight search engines for the best prices. When it comes to food, Priyanka says, "If I'm staying with a friend or at an Airbnb, I usually go to the local market and buy groceries so I can make my own. Street food is also a tasty and budget-friendly option and is safe as long as you know how the street vendors are preparing your food." Priyanka and I agree that the value in traveling has little to do with the luxury—or lack of luxury—in your accommodations and everything to do with the people you interact with and the destination itself.

BOYCOTT
B.D.S.

Boycott, Divestment, Sanctions movement.

Boycotting is familiar to Palestinians. Palestinians depend on many Israeli products. They might not have the resources to create their own. Yet, many Palestinians and pro-Palestinians chose to boycott Israeli products as a form of protest against the inhumanity of Israel.

USE SOCIAL MEDIA

Do your research. Openly receive knowledge. Then, educate and raise awareness. If you have a large following on social media, use your platform to amplify the voices of those who advocate for diversity and tolerance.

VOLUNTEER

Volunteering gives you that chance to physically do something. Action. It does not necessarily illuminate a problem to its root, but it does make a change. Some of my favorite moments in life were in a food bank sorting food with my MEPI student leader friends.

PARTICIPATE IN WEBINARS

In the age of Zoom, Google Meet, and Cisco Webex, if you have high-speed broadband and a computer or mobile device with a camera, you can attend workshops and conferences without leaving home. And with some ingenuity, you can organize and host virtual events, too. It does not have to be formal or high tech. If your purpose is to raise awareness, advocate, call for a boycott, or promote a cause, you may find that Instagram or Facebook Live, for example, offer everything you need.

Workshops can be time-consuming to organize and facilitate but effective and worthwhile when you get it right. Based on my personal experience in workshop development and implementation, participating in one workshop is not sufficient.

Remember that if hosting your own webinar or workshop sounds too stressful or overwhelming, you can make a difference by speaking at someone else's virtual event or simply by participating.

DONATE OR FUNDRAISE

Donating is important. But it is not about how good it makes you feel. If we cannot change the system, then give to those in need—to those neglected by the system.

Some are more privileged than others. In this case, donating a small amount makes a difference. If a hundred thousand people donate ten dollars to a cause, that is a million dollars. A man once asked for people to donate one dollar so he can buy a house. He ended up raising $200,000. That is exactly how one of my previous roommates paid for her ticket. She requested one dollar from her friends on the Venmo app. Even I published this book through crowdfunding. Without my supporters and donors, I would not have reached my publishing goal.

It is the power of numbers.

You don't want to donate? You could always fundraise. Meredith White, the author of *The Fundraiser*, once told me, "Fundraising teaches people the art of giving."

BE CREATIVE

It is not about how you do it; it is about doing it. Do what suits you best and give in-kind. For example, I have recently seen a video of a tattoo artist who removes racist tattoos for free. It is convenient for a tattoo artist. And, it does have a positive impact on those who wish for a fresh, unbiased start. In another video, a dentist offered free braces, on one condition, for a fourteen-year-old girl bullied for her crooked teeth: she pays it forward through being nice rather than mean like her bullies.

The social aspect is important in what we do.

If you are a writer, make a change through your writing.

If you are a singer, sing for social justice.

If you are an artist, draw.

If you are a dancer, dance.

If you are a creator, develop programs and nonprofits.

If you are a leader, start campaigns.

If you are a speaker, give a powerful, well-informed speech.

If you are a fighter, "burn sh*t down," as Anna says.

Use your talents to make a difference.

Do it with love.

And, have hope.

If we want change, we can make it.

TAKEAWAYS

- The main positive aspects of Palestinian culture are unconditional caring and extraordinary hospitality.

- Change begins on a personal level.

- Change is achieved by paying it forward, random acts of kindness, advocacy, traveling, boycotting, using social media to our advantage, participating in webinars, donating and fundraising, and through our many talents.

ACKNOWLEDGMENTS

A book is like a bright moon on a starry night. The supporters are the stars, and the moon is more beautiful in the midst of them.

I would like to thank my sister, Joyce, who inspires me to be a better person every day. I can't wait to see you do more than I do. To my friends, Jowana, Naomi, Ryan, Rama, and Nura, I would have let my stress eat me out without your motivation. Your ongoing support keeps me going. I hold you all very close to my heart.

I am thankful to the Evangelical Lutheran Church in Jordan and the Holy Land. Your generous contribution got me to my publishing goal. To the Evangelical Lutheran Church in America, I wouldn't have been given the chance to write this book without the dreamy opportunities you have given me.

My interviewees, I appreciate you sharing your poignant stories and time.

A special thanks to my wonderful team at New Degree Press, Eric Koester, Brian Bies, Pea Richelle White, and Carol

Thompson. I appreciate you dealing with my Arabic translation to English. I would not have figured it out without your fresh eyes and ideas.

Lastly, thank you to my Beta Readers, who blindly backed this project with love. You helped me become a published author, and your feedback put me on track.

Evangelical Lutheran Church in Jordan and the Holy Land

Lindsey Schillo

Katelyn Robinson

Souha Ouassou

Rama Youssef

Ryan LeGault

Salma Iraqi

Joyce Haddad

Amjaad Shaar

Dr. Rod & Sharon Schofield

Xavier Abu Eid

Nancy Tupper

Paul Witman

Carol & Wolfgang Schmachtel

Robert Pecchio

Leticia Milla

Betty Heusser

Carol Yee

Nada Qaraeen

Nakunda Mshana

Mike Panesis

Rita Tawil

Munther Isaac

Samantha Ea

Carol Gabrielli

Melanie Destoches

Jowana Rinawi

Thea Holtlund

Naomi Mbise

Brittany Toney

Nicola Darwish

Grace Muchahary

Eleanor Barker

Marina Fomgbami

Emmalee Villafana

Carol Schmachtel

Reem Bazbaz

Ranya Rabadi

Eric Koester

Evangelical Lutheran
Church in America

Kassandra Diaz

Mitchel Diggs

Dane Rowley

Rahel Williams

Cortni Kaufman

Kerstin Westerlund

Nicholas D'Souza

Alan Dowzall

Nura Khatib

Zeinab Serhan

Tiki van Heest

Emily Yamamoto

Diana Fielding

Gerhard Apfelthaler

Bobbi Virta

Paul Kellogg

Marta L Hand

Mary Mobley

Cecilia Samuelsson

Christopher Shirley

Paul Silva

Kira Daehlin

Antonia Wada

Carlie Chase

Hanin Salameh

Kaleb Sutherland

Tammy Jackson

Adamik Zsofia

Laurie Parrish

Kristin Bell

Kim Nakano

Christine Cruz

Asi Sitinjak

Jesus & Ana Raya

Haylee Weber

Melissa Maxwell-Doherty

Marian bahbah

Nissa Rolf

Catalina Rodriguez Tapia

Hazel Salazar-Davidson

Caroline Laubach

Tracie Zoom

Catalina Rodriguez Tapia

Greg Monterrosa

Ebrahim Albishri

Scarlet & Salameh Bishara

Seungryeol Yun
& Hannah Ryu

Heidi Vass

Richard Neve

Rishabh Sarin

Adriana Dominguez

Christina Sanchez

Olivia Becker

Priyanka Surio

Mercy Zou

Yen Pham

Hester Foo

Yoshika Masuda

Timar Zsuzsanna

Ftoon AlThaedi

Gia Acosta

Vernon Caraway

Hazar Jaber

Alexander Musleh

Satta Sheriff

jessica Helms

Meriem Mechehoud

Kayomi Kayoshi

Rosie Baker

Mahdi Harmouch

Jwana Nassar

Casey Meyers

Hiba Awad

Daniel Tran

Lena Shinlak

Oliver Riveda

Jonah Gellman

Imane Larousni

Erin Carampot

Zainab Hasan

Demi Wai

Sua Cho

Bliss Tungnung

Leen Hadweh

Celeste Adler

Ann Hightower

Nathan Delacth

Evelina Chandran

Melanie Csellak

Faye Lee

Dalia Jamal Alkhatib

Lara Kasbari

Deena Bregheith

Hellen Rios Carrillo

Pam Henkel

Angela Lotus Qassis

Haley Newlin

Laila Abuayyash

Chuck Sandy

Jamil Khader

Noor Almulla

Stephen Press

Carolina Groff Hinojosa

Ben Sassoon

Ramsey Barghouti

Theodore Casser

Manaf Alomani

Tarik L

Renee King

Mohammad Yacoub

Jeanette Oberhofer

APPENDIX

INTRODUCTION:

ACLU. "End the Use of Religion to Discriminate." *American Civil Liberties Union*, May 19, 2016. https://www.aclu.org/issues/religious-liberty/using-religion-discriminate/end-use-religion-discriminate.

Edwards, Frank, Hedwig Lee, and Michael Esposito. "Risk of Being Killed by Police Use of Force in the United States by Age, Race–Ethnicity, and Sex." *PNAS*, August 20, 2019. https://www.pnas.org/content/116/34/16793.

Ghrayeb, Israa. "التسجيلات الصوتية المحذوفة - بين اسراء غريب وبنت عمها ريهام وشو انحكى على بنت عمها؟" Nour Al Kaddah, Aug 31, 2019. YouTube video, 2:42. https://www.youtube.com/watch?v=KEgLxz3ljMQ&feature=youtu.be.

Merriam Webster. s.v. "Honor Killing." Accessed September 25, 2020. https://www.merriam-webster.com/dictionary/honor%20killing.

Palestinian Central Bureau of Statistics. *الفلسطينيون في نهاية عام 2018*. The State of Palestine: PCBS, 2018. http://www.pcbs.gov.ps/Downloads/book2400.pdf.

Peer, Andrea. "Global Poverty: Facts, FAQs, and How to Help." *World Vision*, June 11, 2020. https://www.worldvision.org/sponsorship-news-stories/global-poverty-facts.

Power, Susan. *Annexing Energy: Exploiting and Preventing the Development of Oil and Gas in the Occupied Palestinian Territory*. Ramallah: Al-Haq, 2015.

Said, Edward W. *Orientalism*. London: Routledge and Kegan Paul, 1978.

Sawafta, Ali. "Palestinian Women Demand Legal Protection after Suspected 'Honor Killing.'" *Reuters*, September 4, 2019. https://www.reuters.com/article/us-palestinians-women-killings/palestinian-women-demand-legal-protection-after-suspected-honor-killing-idUSKCN1VP2AW.

Shalhoub-Kevorkian, Nadera. "Femicide and the Palestinian Criminal Justice System: Seeds of Change in the Context of State Building?" *Law & Society Review* 36, no. 3 (2002): 577. https://doi.org/10.2307/1512163.

The Trevor Project. "Facts About Suicide." September 20, 2017. Accessed June 14, 2020.
https://www.thetrevorproject.org/resources/preventing-suicide/facts-about-suicide/.

Wattad, Muhammad. "النائب العام الفلسطيني: إسراء غريب قتلت نتيجة الضرب." *Arab 48*, September 12, 2019.
https://www.arab48.com/النائب-العام-الفلسطيني-إسراء-غريب-قتلت-/21/90/9102/أخبار/اخبار-عاجلة/
نتيجة-الضرب.

World Bank. "Poverty: Overview." April 16, 2020. Accessed September 15, 2020.
https://www.worldbank.org/en/topic/poverty/overview.

CHAPTER 1:

AJ+. "Why Arabs And Muslims Aren't Exotic." December 10, 2017. Video, 9:39.
https://www.youtube.com/watch?v=ddCJPtcxEwo.

"Aladdin," *Disney*, produced by Walt Disney Feature Animation (Burbank, CA: Walt
Disney Pictures, 1992), DVD.

Anne Frank House. "Why Did Hitler Hate the Jews?" June 8, 2020. Accessed
September 16, 2020.
https://www.annefrank.org/en/anne-frank/go-in-depth/why-did-hitler-hate-jews/.

"A Quote by Edward W. Said." *Goodreads*. Accessed October 3, 2020.
https://www.goodreads.com/quotes/356323-you-cannot-continue-to-victimize-
someone-else-just-because-you.

B'Tselem. "Israel's Control of the Airspace and the Territorial Waters of the Gaza
Strip." Accessed September 18, 2020.
https://www.btselem.org/gaza_strip/control_on_air_space_and_territorial_waters.

Dawson, Geoffrey. "Palestine for the Jews." *The Times of London*, 9 November, 1917.

Herzl, Theodor. *The Jewish State*. New York: Dover Publications, Inc., 2008.

History.com Editors. "Palestine." *History*. A&E Television Networks, August 11, 2017.
https://www.history.com/topics/middle-east/palestine.

Holocaust Encyclopedia, s.v. "Who were the Victims?" Washington DC: United
States Holocaust Memorial Museum, 2020. Accessed September 16, 2020.
https://encyclopedia.ushmm.org/content/en/article/mosaic-of-victims-an-overview.

National Geographic. "National Geographic Documentary 2015—Albert Einstein—
How I See The World." World Documentaries. April 8, 2015. YouTube video, 1:34:02.
https://www.youtube.com/watch?v=OBmP_7k2h_4.

Rouyer, Alwyn R. "The Water Accords of Oslo II: Averting a Looming
Disaster." *Middle East Policy Council*, 1999.
https://mepc.org/journal/water-accords-oslo-ii-averting-looming-disaster.

Shawky, Sarah Ahmed. "Once upon a Time, Palestine Had Its Own Int'l Airport ...
but It Was Short-Lived." *StepFeed*, April 12, 2017. Accessed September 16, 2020.
https://stepfeed.com/once-upon-a-time-palestine-had-its-own-int-l-airport-but-it-
was-short-lived-1105.

CHAPTER 2:

Abunimah, Ali. "Video: Israeli Soldier Forces Knife on Palestinian Girl." *The Electronic Intifada*, December 2, 2015. https://electronicintifada.net/blogs/ali-abunimah/video-israeli-soldier-forces-knife-palestinian-girl.

Al Jazeera. "Israel Admits Holding Body of Palestinian Killed in West Bank." October 9, 2020. https://www.aljazeera.com/news/2020/10/9/israel-says-holding-body-of-palestinian-killed-in-west-bank.

"Chapter 3: Israeli Settlements and International Law." Amnesty International. Accessed October 18, 2020. https://www.amnesty.org/en/latest/campaigns/2019/01/chapter-3-israeli-settlements-and-international-law/.

"Chomsky on Palestinian Unpeople." *Antony Loewenstein (blog).* October 19, 2011. Accessed September 21, 2020. https://antonyloewenstein.com/chomsky-on-palestinian-unpeople/.

Collier, David. "Banksy West Bank Bethlehem Hotel Review: An Antisemitic Sham." *The David Collier blog (blog),* May 10, 2018. http://david-collier.com/banksy-bethlehem/.

Cook, Jonathan. "Inside Banksy's The Walled Off Hotel in Bethlehem." The National. December 22, 2018. https://www.thenationalnews.com/arts-culture/inside-banksy-s-the-walled-off-hotel-in-bethlehem-1.804845.

Fawcett, Harry. "Anger at Killing of Autistic Palestinian by Israeli Police." *Al Jazeera,* June 2, 2020. https://www.aljazeera.com/videos/2020/06/02/anger-at-killing-of-autistic-palestinian-by-israeli-police/.

Garrigues, Lisa Gale, and Lisa Gale Garrigues. "Slave and Slaveholder Descendants Break Free of History's Trauma-Together." Yes! Magazine, August 3, 2013. https://www.yesmagazine.org/issue/love-apocalypse/2013/08/03/free-yourself-from-the-past/.

Haaretz. "New Poll Shows Atheism on Rise, with Jews Found to Be Least Religious." January 11, 2018. https://www.haaretz.com/jewish/jews-least-observant-int-l-poll-finds-1.5287579.

Khader, Jamil. "Architectural Parallax, Neoliberal Politics and the Universality of the Palestinian Struggle: Banksy's Walled Off Hotel." *European Journal of Cultural Studies* 23, no. 3 (2020): 474–94. https://doi.org/10.1177/1367549420902787.

Khoury, Jack, Yaniv Kubovich, and Hagar Shezaf. "Palestinian Shot Dead by Israeli Forces; Army Says He Threw Firebombs at Soldiers." Haaretz.com. October 5, 2020. https://www.haaretz.com/israel-news/.premium-palestinian-shot-dead-by-israeli-forces-army-says-he-threw-firebombs-at-soldiers-1.9210988.

Salman, Abeer, and Andrew Carey. "Unarmed Palestinian Man Shot Dead by Police in Jerusalem." CNN. Cable News Network, May 31, 2020. https://www.cnn.com/2020/05/30/middleeast/unarmed-palestinian-killed-jerusalem-intl/index.html.

Salsa, Reuben. "11 Best COVID-19 Protest Signs." Medium. Better Marketing, April 23, 2020. https://medium.com/better-marketing/11-best-covid-19-protest-signs-4e7ebacdcfa7.

The New Arab Staff & Agencies. "Israeli Police Hold Palestinian Man over Knife Killing." *The New Arab*, August 26, 2020. https://english.alaraby.co.uk/english/news/2020/8/26/israeli-police-hold-palestinian-man-over-knife-killing.

Victor Diab. "Victor Diab and Jamil Khader." May 25, 2020. Video, 1:03:03. https://www.youtube.com/watch?v=pmFdBiiu5O8&feature=youtu.be&fbclid=IwAR16_De9t7MjUyuCpOEmeiWi4BoiMjo81ePJ9jK2hOd3GYpJKEHvvj7QF44

70SHARESAVE.

Yansori, Ali. "The Concept of Trauma in Lacanian Psychoanalysis." *Psychoanalýza dnes*. December 25, 2018. http://psychoanalyzadnes.cz/2018/02/19/the-concept-of-trauma-in-lacanian-psychoanalysis/.

CHAPTER 3:

Garfinkle, Adam M. "On the Origin, Meaning, Use and Abuse of a Phrase." Middle Eastern Studies 27, no. 4 (1991): 539-50. Accessed September 30, 2020. http://www.jstor.org/stable/4283461.

Hatem Bazian. "Dr. Hatem Bazian Conversation with Professor Jamil Khader, Dean of Research at Bethlehem University." October 3, 2020. Video. 1:22:56. https://www.youtube.com/watch?v=ikNWjrCD3_o&feature=youtu.be

"Identity." Psychology Today. Accessed October 6, 2020. https://www.psychologytoday.com/us/basics/identity.

Internet Encyclopedia of Philosophy. s.v. "Jacques Lacan." Accessed October 5, 2020. https://iep.utm.edu/lacweb/

Khader, Jamil. "Architectural Parallax, Neoliberal Politics and the Universality of the Palestinian Struggle: Banksy's Walled Off Hotel." *European Journal of Cultural Studies* 23, no. 3 (2020): 474–94. https://doi.org/10.1177/1367549420902787.

Maalouf, Amin. *In the Name of identity: Violence and the Need to Belong*. Translated by Barbara Bray. New York: Penguin Books, 2000).

Merriam Webster. s.v. "Concrete Universal." Accessed October 5, 2020. https://www.merriam-webster.com/dictionary/concrete%20universal

"Palestine Refugees: Locations and Numbers." The New Humanitarian, January 17, 2018. Accessed September 22, 2020. https://www.thenewhumanitarian.org/report/89571/middle-east-palestinian-refugee-numberswhereabouts.

"Palestine Refugees." UNRWA. Accessed September 22, 2020. https://www.unrwa.org/palestine-refugees.

Pfeiffer, Michaela V., *Vulnerability and the International Health Response in the West Bank and Gaza Strip: an Analysis of Health and the Health Sector.* Jerusalem: World Health Organization, 2001. Accessed September 21, 2020.

Salam, Ali. "31 Years Ago, Arafat Declared Independence of the State of Palestine." *IMEMC News,* November 14, 2019. https://imemc.org/article/31-years-ago-arafat-declared-independence-of-the-state-of-palestine/.

The Japan Times. "The Annexation of Korea." August 29, 2010. https://www.japantimes.co.jp/opinion/2010/08/29/editorials/the-annexation-of-korea/.

Wilkinson, Ron. "Where Are the Tents? It Is a Camp, Isn't It?" *BADIL Resource Center for Palestinian Residency and Refugee Rights.* Accessed September 22, 2020. https://www.badil.org/en/publication/periodicals/al-majdal/item/907-where-are-the-tents.

CHAPTER 4

"الودود الولود في ميزان العدل الرباني." جريدة الدستور الاردنية". Accessed September 23, 2020. https://www.addustour.com/articles/930808-%D8%A7%D9%84%D9%88%D8%AF%D9%88%D8%AF-%D8%A7%D9%84%D9%88%D9%84%D9%88%D8%AF-%D9%81%D9%8A-%D9%85%D9%8A%D8%B2%D8%A7%D9%86-%D8%A7%D9%84-4%D8%B9%D8%AF%D9%84-%D8%A7%D9%84%D8%B1%D8%A8%D8%A7%D9%86%D9%8A.

"A/RES/67/19 of 4 December 2012." *United Nations.* Accessed September 22, 2020. https://unispal.un.org/UNISPAL.NSF/0/19862D03C564FA2C85257ACB004EE69B.

"An Overview of ISIS." Islamic Networks Group (ING). Accessed September 22, 2020. https://ing.org/an-overview-of-isis/.

Ashcroft, Bill, Gareth Griffiths, and Helen Tiffin. *Post-Colonial Studies: The Key Concepts.* London: Routledge, 2007.

Bailey, Randall C. "The Bible as a text of Cultures." *The People's Bible,* edited by Paul DeYoung, Curtiss, Wilda C. Gafney, Leticia A. Guardiola-Saens, George "Tink" Tinker, and Frank M. Yamada (Minneapolis: Fortress Press, 2009), 13–22.

Burkholder, James Peter., Donald Jay Grout, and Claude Victor. Palisca. *A History of Western Music.* New York: W.W. Norton and Company, 2019.

Encyclopaedia Britannica. s.v. "Pharisee." Accessed September 21, 2020. https://www.britannica.com/topic/Pharisee.

Hodge, Bodie. "How Old Is the Earth?" Answers in Genesis, May 30, 2007. https://answersingenesis.org/age-of-the-earth/how-old-is-the-earth/.

Patterson, Claire. "Age of Meteorites and the Earth." *Geochimica et Cosmochimica Acta* 10, no. 4 (1956): 230–37. https://doi.org/10.1016/0016-7037(56)90036-9.

"Religious Composition by Country, 2010-2050." Pew Research Center's Religion & Public Life Project. Accessed September 21, 2020. https://www.pewforum.org/2015/04/02/religious-projection-table/2020/percent/all/.

"Self-Determination." UNPO. Accessed September 22, 2020. https://unpo.org/article/4957.

Stanford Encyclopedia of Philosophy. s.v. "Nationalism." Accessed September 21, 2020. https://plato.stanford.edu/entries/nationalism/.

TED. "What does the Quran really say about a Muslim woman's hijab?" Feb 10, 2017. Video, 17:47. https://www.youtube.com/watch?v=_J5bDhMP9lQ.

"The Rise of Islamic Empires and States (Article)." Khan Academy. Khan Academy. Accessed September 22, 2020. https://www.khanacademy.org/humanities/world-history/medieval-times/spread-of-islam/a/the-rise-of-islamic-empires-and-states.

Throop, Susanna. "The Impact of the Crusades." Smarthistory. Accessed September 22, 2020. https://smarthistory.org/the-impact-of-the-crusades-4-of-4/.

Unorthodox. Directed by Maria Schrader. Written by Anna Winger, Alexa Karolinski, and Daniel Hendler, inspired by Deborah Feldman's 2012 autobiography. Debuted on March 26, 2020, on Netflix.

Victor Diab. "Victor Diab and Jamil Khader." May 25, 2020. Video, 1:03:03. https://www.youtube.com/watch?v=pmFdBiiu5O8&feature=youtu.be&fbclid=IwAR16_De9t7MjUyuCpOEmeiWi4B0iMj081ePJ9jK2hOd3GYpJKEHvvj7QF44

70SHARESAVE.

CHAPTER 5

Beauvoir, Simone De. *The Second Sex.* Translated by Constance Borde and Sheila Malovany Chevallier. New York: Vintage, 2011.

Beauvoir, Simone De. *The Second Sex.* Translated by H. M. Parshley. New York: Alfred A. Knopf, 1953.

Beauvoir, Simone De. "The Second Sex." *Vintage Classic* 3.no. 1 (2011). https://libcom.org/files/1949_simone-de-beauvoir-the-second-sex.pdf

International Labour Organization. "Exploring the gender pay gap in Occupied Palestinian Territory: A qualitative study of the education sector." *Policy Brief 2016.* *https://www.ilo.org/wcmsp5/groups/public/---arabstates/---ro-beirut/documents/publication/wcms_542472.pdf*

Raheb, Mitri. *Middle Eastern Women: The Intersection of Law, Culture, and Religion.* Bethlehem: Diyar Publisher, 2020).

UN Women Palestine. "Facts and Figures: Ending Violence against Women." Accessed October 3, 2020. https://palestine.unwomen.org/en/what-we-do/ending-violence-against-women/facts-and-figures.

WikiMiki. "Education in the State of Palestine." Accessed October 3, 2020. https://wikimili.com/en/Education_in_the_State_of_Palestine

CHAPTER 6

AP Archive. "Jerusalem's Afro Palestinians feel more integrated." Feb 5, 2017. video, 4:25.
https://www.youtube.com/watch?v=aOnL8oyhiko&t=63s

Baker, Joharah. "The African-Palestinians: Muslim Pilgrims Who Never Went
Home." *The New Arab*, December 26, 2014.
https://english.alaraby.co.uk/english/features/2014/12/26/the-african-palestinians-
muslim-pilgrims-who-never-went-home.

Bivens, Donna. "What Is Internalized Racism?" *Flipping the Script: White Privilege
and Community Building*, 43-52. United States: MP Associates, Inc., 2005.

"Blackface: The Birth of An American Stereotype." *National Museum of African
American History and Culture*, November 22, 2017.
https://nmaahc.si.edu/blog-post/blackface-birth-american-stereotype.

"Is There Meaningful Debate to Be Had about Banning the n-Word? | The N-Word
Project." *The Washington Post*. Accessed September 30, 2020.
https://www.washingtonpost.com/video/national/is-there-meaningful-debate-to-
be-had-about-banning-the-n-word--the-n-word-project/2018/12/28/849d3dbf-81d1-
4ef4-a5fd-a74b1f8dae55_video.html.

Khaled, Maryam Abu (@maryamabukhaled1). "العنصرية الغير مقصودة والغير مباشرة بعد معنا
وقت." Instagram photo, June 5, 2020,
https://www.instagram.com/tv/CBDz58CHRlj/?igshid=18ct28pud4rs1.

Khaled, Maryam Abu (@maryamabukhaled1). "حبايبي ديرو بالكم بطريقة التضامن لأنو مرات بتكون
عكسية ما تكونوا متل هاي الناس كل الناس خير وبركة صباحكم عسل." Instagram photo, June 3, 2020,
https://www.instagram.com/p/CA96FHFnFoJ/?utm_source=ig_web_copy_link

King, Wyman, Richard C. Emanuel, Xavier Brown, Niroby Dingle, Vertis
Lucas, Anissa Perkins, Ayzia Turner, Destinee Whittington, and Qwa'dryna
Witherspoon. "Who has the 'Right' to Use the N-Word? A Survey of Attitudes about
the Acceptability of Using the N-Word and its Derivatives." *International Journal of
Society, Culture &Language* 6, no.2 (September 2018): 47–58.

Lyman, Stanford M. "The 'Yellow Peril' Mystique: Origins and Vicissitudes of a
Racist Discourse." *International Journal of Politics, Culture, and Society* 13, no. 4
(2000): 683–747.
https://www.jstor.org/stable/20020056

Lewis, Thomas. s.v. "Transatlantic Slave Trade." *Encyclopedia Britannica*, April 6, 2020.
https://www.britannica.com/topic/transatlantic-slave-trade.

Merriam Webster. s.v. "Xenophobia." Accessed September 30, 2020.
https://www.merriam-webster.com/dictionary/xenophobia

"New Fertility Procedure Allows 2 Women to Carry Same Baby, Presents New
Choices for Same-Sex Couples." ABC7 San Francisco. October 29, 2018.
https://abc7news.com/two-moms-mothers-pregnancy-carry-same-baby/4576470/.

"Racism." Anti-Defamation League. Accessed September 28, 2020.
https://www.adl.org/racism.

Seitz, Charmaine."Pilgrimage to a New Self: The African Quarter and its
people." *Institute for Palestine Studies*, no. 16 (2020): 43.
https://oldwebsite.palestine-studies.org/jq/fulltext/78020

Starkey, Brando. "If You Truly Knew What the N-Word Meant to Our Ancestors, You'd Never Use It." *The Undefeated*, May 18, 2017. https://theundefeated.com/features/if-you-truly-knew-what-the-n-word-meant-to-our-ancestors-youd-never-use-it/.

"The Theory of Yellow Peril." Study.com. Accessed October 1, 2020. https://study.com/academy/lesson/the-theory-of-yellow-peril.html.

Tim J. Wise, *Speaking Treason Fluently: Anti-Racist Reflections From an Angry White Male* (Brooklyn: Soft Skull Press, 2008).

X, Malcolm, and Steve Clark. *By Any Means Necessary*. New York: Pathfinder, 2019.

Zheng, Robin. "Why Yellow Fever Isn't Flattering: A Case Against Racial Fetishes." *Cambridge University Press* 2, no. 3 (October 2016): 400-419. https://doi.org/10.1017/apa.2016.25

Zion, Ilan Ben. "The Old City's African Secret." *The Times of Israel*, April 6, 2014. https://www.timesofisrael.com/the-old-citys-african-secret/#gs.f9d414

CHAPTER 7

Abrams, Mere. "46 Terms That Describe Sexual Attraction, Behavior & Orientation." *Healthline*, December 10, 2019. https://www.healthline.com/health/different-types-of-sexuality.

"Boomers, Gen X, Gen Y, and Gen Z Explained." *Kasasa*. Accessed October 1, 2020. https://www.kasasa.com/articles/generations/gen-x-gen-y-gen-z.

Brabaw, Kasandra. "Allosexual, Demisexual, Bicurious-& Other Sexualities You Need To Know." *Refinery 29*. Accessed October 1, 2020. https://www.refinery29.com/en-us/sexual-orientation-types-of-sexualities.

Butler, Judith. "Imitation and Gender Insubordination." *The Lesbian and Gay Studies Reader*, edited by Henry Abelove, Michele Aina Barale, and David M. Halperin, 306- 320. New York: Routledge, 1993.

"Egyptian LGBT activist dies by suicide in Canada." *Aljazeera*, June 15, 2020. https://www.aljazeera.com/news/2020/06/15/egyptian-lgbt-activist-dies-by-suicide-in-canada/

Qazi, Moin. *Women In Islam- Exploring New Paradigms*. Triplicane: Notion Press, 2015.

Rebel News. "Shunned: A film about LGBT Palestinians in Israel." July 6, 2015. Video, 50:14. https://www.youtube.com/watch?v=I4dLMtF7s9U

Rudgard, Olivia. "Only Two-Thirds of Generation Z Identify as 'Exclusively Heterosexual.'" *The Telegraph*, July 5, 2018. https://www.telegraph.co.uk/news/2018/07/05/two-thirds-generation-z-identify-exclusively-heterosexual/.

"Same Sex Parents and Their Children." American Association for Marriage and Family Therapy. Accessed October 1, 2020. https://www.aamft.org/Consumer_Updates/Same-sex_Parents_and_Their_Children.aspx.

"Sexual Attraction and Orientation." *Teens Health from Nemours*. Accessed October 1, 2020. https://kidshealth.org/en/teens/sexual-orientation.html.

Stein, Abby. *Becoming Eve My Journey from Ultra-Orthodox Rabbi to Transgender Woman*. New York: Seal Press, 2019.

The Forge Online. "Has 'Homosexual' Always Been in the Bible?" *United Methodist Insight*, October 14, 2019. https://um-insight.net/perspectives/has-%E2%80%9Chomosexual%E2%80%9D-always-been-in-the-bible/.

Walsh, Declan. "Arrested for Waving Rainbow Flag, a Gay Egyptian Takes Her Life." *The New York Times*, June 15, 2020. https://www.nytimes.com/2020/06/15/world/middleeast/egypt-gay-suicide-sarah-hegazi.html.

"What Is Intersex?: Definition of Intersexual." *Planned Parenthood*. Accessed October 1, 2020. https://www.plannedparenthood.org/learn/gender-identity/sex-gender-identity/whats-intersex.

CHAPTER 8

Andino, Sgt. Ana. "Latest Lesson in Human Trafficking Features More than Just Sex Slaves; How about Cases of Organ Harvesting." Houston Police Officers' Union. Accessed October 26, 2020. https://hpou.org/latest-lesson-in-human-trafficking-features-more-than-just-sex-slaves-how-about-cases-of-organ-harvesting/.

Big Think. "Slavoj Žižek: Democracy and Capitalism Are Destined to Split Up." January 7, 2015. Video, 17:19. https://www.youtube.com/watch?v=AXVEnxtZe_w&feature=youtu.be

Bruenig, Elizabeth. "Gods and Profits." *The New Republic*, April 20, 2015. https://newrepublic.com/article/121564/gods-and-profits-how-capitalism-and-christianity-aligned-america.

Buchanan, Larry, Quoctrung Bui, and Jugal K. Patel. "Black Lives Matter May Be the Largest Movement in US History." *The New York Times*. July 3, 2020. https://www.nytimes.com/interactive/2020/07/03/us/george-floyd-protests-crowd-size.html.

Dictionary.com. s.v. "Femicide." Accessed October 4, 2020. https://www.dictionary.com/browse/femicide

Fessler, Pam. "US Census Bureau Reports Poverty Rate Down, But Millions Still Poor." NPR. September 10, 2019. https://www.npr.org/2019/09/10/759512938/u-s-census-bureau-reports-poverty-rate-down-but-millions-still-poor.

Hamilton, Isobel Asher. "Twitter Slapped a 'Glorifying Violence' Label on a Trump Tweet That Threatened George Floyd Protesters in Minneapolis with Getting Shot." Business Insider. May 29, 2020. https://www.businessinsider.com/twitter-warning-trump-tweet-george-floyd-glorifying-violence-2020-5.

"Israel." 2020 Index of Economic Freedom. Accessed October 17, 2020. https://www.heritage.org/index/country/israel.

Jeffrey Epstein: Filthy Rich. Directed by Lisa Bryant. Aired May 27, 2020 on Netflix.

Kadman, Noga. "Employment of Palestinians in Israel and the Settlements: Restrictive Policies and Abuse of Rights." *Kav LaOved,* 2012. https://palestinakomiteen.no/wp-content/uploads/2013/05/employment-of-palestinians-in-Israel.pdf

Khader, Jamil. "Architectural Parallax, Neoliberal Politics and the Universality of the Palestinian Struggle: Banksy's Walled Off Hotel." *European Journal of Cultural Studies* 23, no. 3 (2020): 474–94. https://doi.org/10.1177/1367549420902787.

Khader, Jamil. "The Invisible Link: Honor Killing and Global Capitalism." *Jadaliyya* 3, no.1 (January 2013).

Martin, Douglas. "Saudi Arabia's New Capitalism." The New York Times. February 21, 1982. https://www.nytimes.com/1982/02/21/business/saudi-arabia-s-new-capitalism.html.

Marx, Karl, and Friedrich Engels. "Economic and Philosophic Manuscripts of 1844." 1956.

Mastersofscale. "The Next Silicon Valley: Linda Rottenberg on Masters of Scale." January 30, 2020. https://mastersofscale.com/linda-rottenberg-the-next-silicon-valley/.

New Internationalist. "The Interview: Slavoj Žižek." May 3, 2019. https://newint.org/features/2019/02/11/interview-Slavoj-Zizek.

NowThis News. "AOC Calls Out Billionaires at MLK Day Event." January 24, 2020. Video, 4:22. https://www.youtube.com/watch?v=lAnRUepeb_U&feature=youtu.be

Poets.org. "On Children by Kahlil Gibran - Poems | Academy of American Poets." Accessed October 4, 2020. https://poets.org/poem/children-1.

Robert Reich (@RBReich). "Your reminder that America's richest 1 percent now own half the value of the US stock market." Twitter, July 5, 2020, 4:44 p.m. https://twitter.com/RBReich/status/1279924108411596802

Robinson, William I. "Global Capitalism: Crisis of Humanity and the Specter of 21st Century Fascism." *The world Financial Review.* May 27, 2014. https://worldfinancialreview.com/global-capitalism-crisis-humanity-specter-21st-century-fascism

Speculative Realism. "Žižek! [Full Movie | 2005]." September 18, 2019. Video, 55:46. https://www.youtube.com/watch?v=5brjo5XehVk

Tedbundystuff. "Ted Bundy Documentary - Death Row Tapes (Full)." February 21, 2017. Video, 43:58. https://www.youtube.com/watch?v=_et_67Epyuk

"US Relations With Saudi Arabia." US Department of State. November 26, 2019. https://www.state.gov/u-s-relations-with-saudi-arabia/.

Vatter, Miguel, ed. *Crediting God: Sovereignty and Religion in the Age of Global Capitalism.* New York: Fordham University Press, 2011. Accessed October 17, 2020. doi:10.2307/j.ctt13x026n.

CHAPTER 9

Aronson, Brittany A. "The White Savior Industrial Complex: A Cultural Studies Analysis of a Teacher Educator, Savior Film, and Future Teachers." *Journal of critical Thought and Praxis* 6, no.3 (2017): 36-54.

Cole, Teju. "The White-Savior Industrial Complex." *The Atlantic*, January 11, 2013. https://www.theatlantic.com/international/archive/2012/03/the-white-savior-industrial-complex/254843/.

Grant, Adam. *Give and Take: a Revolutionary Approach to Success.* London: Weidenfeld & Nicolson, 2014.

Kai, Christopher. "Tamar Haddad." May 7, 2019. *Anchor.* Podcast, episode 448, 9:54. https://anchor.fm/thegifters/episodes/Ep--448-Tamar-Haddad-edo5aa/Ep--447-Tamar-Haddad-a24lp4q

Melnyck, Kyrie. "Homelessness in Israel/Palestine." *Homeless Entrepreneur,* February 22, 2017. https://www.homelessentrepreneur.org/en/blog/2018/1/28/homelessness-in-israelpalestine.

"Pay It Forward." *Bel-Air Entertainment.* Directed by Mimi Leder. CA: Warner Bros. Pictures, 2000.

TEDx Talks. "Five steps to becoming an advocate." January 30, 2018. Video, 7:00. https://www.youtube.com/watch?v=nI031mMB4P8

"The American White Savior Complex." Tablet Magazine, June 6, 2019. https://www.tabletmag.com/sections/news/articles/americas-white-saviors.

THE MAP OF PALESTINE

Map of Palestine

✸ Capital

■ Occupied Palestine,
  also known as Israel

West Bank: Administered by
Palestinians Authorities

Gaza Strip: Administered by
Palestinians Authorities

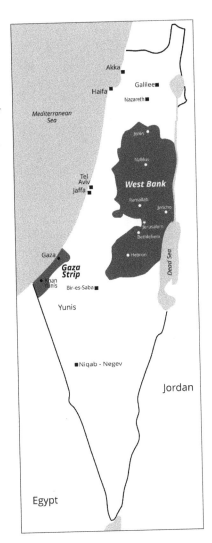

CPSIA information can be obtained
at www.ICGtesting.com
Printed in the USA
FSHW021524201220